DOWNTOWN TURNAROUND

LESSONS FOR A NEW URBAN LANDSCAPE

DANIEL CORT

PARK PLACE PUBLICATIONS
PACIFIC GROVE, CALIFORNIA

Downtown Turnaround
Lessons for a New Urban Landscape

Daniel Cort

First Edition July 2010

© 2010 Daniel E. Cort
With Nina Solomita

All rights reserved. No part of this book may be reproduced by any means whatsoever without written permission from the publisher, except brief portions quoted for purpose of review.

Library of Congress Control Number: 2009931961

ISBN 13: 978-1-935530-01-5

Published by
Park Place Publications
P.O. Box 829
Pacific Grove, CA 93950
www.parkplacepublications.com

Cover design by Michelle Manos
Interior book design by Patricia Hamilton

Special thanks to Randy Tunnell for Stockton and Monterey project photos. Cover photo by Terry Way. Vintage Stockton photos where noted courtesy of the Bank of Stockton Historical Photograph Collection. Additional vintage building photos from Cort Companies archives. Other photo credits: Jupiter Images 1, 9, 13-21; Patricia Hamilton 29, 31, 32, 35, 162, 168, 169, 170, 172, 176, 181, 182, 184, 185; and Sharon Blaziek 161, 163, 178.

Printed in China with vegetable based ink. Our printer meets or exceeds all Federal Resource Conservation Recovery Act (RCRA) Standards. Our printer is a certified member of the Forest Stewardship Council (FSC). The FSC sets high standards that ensure forestry is practiced in an environmentally responsible, socially beneficial and economically viable way.
In addition, one tree for every book printed has been planted through ecolibris.net.

"There is magic to great streets. We are attracted to the best of them not because we have to go there but because we want to be there. The best are as joyful as they are utilitarian. They are entertaining and they are open to all. They permit anonymity at the same time as individual recognition. They are symbols of a community and of its history; they represent a public memory. They are places for escape and for romance, places to act and to dream."
Allan B. Jacobs. *Great Streets*

Lobby of Cort Tower, Stockton.

Contents

Acknowledgments	
Imagine	8
The House of the Future	16
City Planning	26
Urban Building Blocks	34
The Victorians	66
Heritage Square	72
Eden Square	84
Railroad Square	96
Cort Tower	110
600 and 540 East Main	128
The Kress Legal Center and Law Library	146
The Monterey Peninsula	161
Epilogue	188

Dedication

To my wife, Beth, who supported me in this journey of discovery and provided an anchor in the sometimes stormy seas of contra-developing. To my children, Jessica, Zachary, and Joshua, my inspiration for a new town downtown.

Acknowledgments

I have been extremely fortunate to have had the assistance of so many talented, committed colleagues. With great appreciation to Mahala Burns, who always helped create harmonies; Peggy Massey whose assistance was immeasurable in the procurement of historical photos; Howard Burns, who covered the details; Floyd Hall, the one-man public relations department for our company; Ruby Dhillon, our creative IT muse; Robert, Lupe, and all of our talented team in Stockton, Pacific Grove, and the Central Coast. With deep respect and admiration for Nina Solomita and her skill and patience in guiding me through the complex pathways of this book and helping me to open the floodgates of memory. Much gratitude to my publisher and book designer, Patricia Hamilton, who believed in my work and especially in the power of the "story." Thanks to Michelle Manos for her wonderful friendship and artistry in the creation of our cover.

IMAGINE

"The real voyage of discovery consists not in seeking new landscapes, but in seeing with new eyes."
Marcel Proust

You are walking down a familiar city street that once bustled with people shopping, going about business, enjoying the restaurants or a movie at the theater, or heading home after a busy day. Every block holds a memory: The studio where you took ballet lessons; the store where you bagged groceries after school; the movie theater where you went on that awkward first date.

Only now the theater's façade is cracked, the paint is peeling, and the marquee reads "CLOSED." That great breakfast place on the corner is boarded up. This street and its once vibrant buildings—in fact, the whole neighborhood, like others throughout the country—are neglected and abandoned. Rejected by its previous owners who opted for another kind of life in the sprawling suburbs and exurbs, the streets are now the province of the transient, living in flophouses or homeless, victims of poverty, alcohol and drug abuse. Now, imagine zeroing in on one building, that old brick schoolhouse over there covered with graffiti, its windows broken. A sorry sight.

Perhaps you went to that school or know someone who did. What a shame to see it deserted and left to decay, the schoolyard that once teemed with children running and jumping rope now full of weeds, littered with old newspapers and debris. How wasteful that this still-sturdy resource, with its architectural history and, more importantly, its personal history in so many lives, no longer serves a purpose. The reasons for its decline are complex, but it's clear that many of the problems that led to its present state stem from a lack of respect for our heritage and a failure to plan for the future.

But what if, instead of perceiving the situation as hopeless, you identify it as an opportunity? What if you realize that the old school building is brimming with the potential for transformation, which could, in turn, lead the way to a series of transformations in the

> "You never want a serious crisis to go to waste.... It's an opportunity to do things that you thought you could not do before."
>
> Rahm Emanuel,
> Chief of Staff to President Barack Obama

neighborhood? What if you visualize this deteriorated landscape with new eyes, imagine new possibilities—the building restored and repurposed, filled with productive people, an asset to the community? Then, what if you embrace your ability to make a difference—to change a small piece of your world—and take the steps to manifest your vision?

Downtown Turnaround: Lessons for a New Urban Landscape is about hope and opportunity in a time when our country and the world are in the midst of a serious economic, social, and environmental crisis that we cannot afford to let *go to waste*. Global warming is real; the depletion of our natural resources is real; the time we have to turn around the destruction is finite. Inextricably bound in this morass is the mortgage and housing debacle perpetrated by decades of greed, denial, and lack of foresight.

This recession/depression has shocked people into relinquishing long-held views about lifestyles that can no longer be sustained, wasteful practices we can no longer afford. One of the adjustments we must all make will be to become better stewards of the environment—not just because it is the right thing to do, but because it is the socially, economically, and environmentally smart course. We must learn to recycle not just the household garbage, but the beautiful, abandoned assets of our past. Why? Because the way we used to build cities was more environmentally friendly. When services and resources were centralized, energy was used more efficiently. Cheaper energy for transportation led to sprawl, wasteful commutes, and the decline of these once-efficient urban cores.

We don't need to cut down whole forests to build new, when we have wonderful buildings just waiting for a little tender loving care. By reviving these neighborhoods, by bringing back to life the fabulous architecture of our past, we are creating a more sustainable economy. We need to learn to use what we already have in the built environment rather than continue the trend of building out to the suburbs and beyond, where long commutes result in the expansion of our carbon footprint.

The American Institute of Architecture has initiated "Challenge 2030" calling for a 50% reduction in use of fossil fuels for buildings in four years, with additional reductions leading to eventual carbon-neutrality by 2030. "By implementing the Challenge, we can first stabilize, and then begin reducing fossil-fuel energy consumption in the Building Sector. Renovating existing buildings to consume 50 percent less fossil fuel energy allows for new efficient buildings to be built without increasing the sector's energy demand. If we wait, even 10 years, this window of opportunity is lost."

www.architecture2030.org

In Crisis Is Opportunity

Bad as things are today, there is an enormous opportunity for those with imagination to prosper while providing an indispensable service to their communities and, in turn, to the country. We've been in similar circumstances before and can learn from the experience. In fact, when I began my business in architectural preservation in the 1970s, then as today:

- We had just experienced a period of inflated and false prosperity.
- Property values were very low.
- People were unsure about their futures.
- Credit was tight.
- Many properties with potential languished.
- Everyone wanted to save money, but was at a loss about how to do it.
- There were opportunities for innovative partnerships.
- We were focused on green and sustainable building, although the concept and the challenges that defined it, hadn't entered popular usage.

A Clarion Call

Downtown Turnaround is a clarion call to students and professionals in urban development and city planning, architecture, architectural preservation, and sustainability—and to every citizen who wants to improve his or her environment. Its purpose is to inspire you to reclaim urban areas and to create a greener, sustainable future through the built environment by taking action in your neighborhoods and communities.

You can create your fortune—by which I mean your future, your destiny, and your financial reward—while you contribute to re-enlivening our deserted city resources and communities. With an entrepreneurial spirit, you can make money as neighborhoods, towns, and cities are saved. I've done it for the past thirty-five years with my primary objectives being to revitalize city centers and downtown areas and recreate communities.

There are as many ways to impact your environment as there are original and creative thinkers. You don't have to be in a building profession to contribute to saving our cities. Lawyers can negotiate contracts, while politicians can help amend the excessive regulations that discourage renovation of historic architecture. Scientists can educate the public on ways to leave a smaller carbon footprint. Shoppers can buy from small businesses rather than big-box outlets. Teachers and parents can educate children about preserving our natural resources and maintaining a greener lifestyle. Investors, large and small, can participate in specific renovation projects. Grant writers can apply to corporations and foundations for funding. Every citizen can have a voice in local politics.

We can use our voices, our imaginations, our energy, to turn around the destructive path of the past several decades, in which city centers have been abandoned in favor of sprawl. We must save our city centers in order to save our environment, our economy, and ourselves. By describing my unique journey through a system that often doesn't support restorative enterprises, you'll see how one person can make a difference—how *you* can make a difference. *Downtown Turnaround* provides the kind of guidance I would have welcomed as a rookie starting out.

What Do I Know?

It was the early 1970s. I was twenty-three, broke, and had never taken out a loan other than for college. My ability to build or develop a property was completely untested, except for an experiment on a remote river island in the Central Valley of California. Inspired by the restorations of many vivid, colorful Victorians in San Francisco, I decided to buy and renovate a run-down Victorian in Stockton.

In the years since, Cort Companies has restored nearly two million square feet, creating new mixed-use and commercial spaces. We have never built a new structure; our focus is the revitalization of cities and downtown areas, and our properties have served as models for restoration and urban growth. In downtown Stockton, we've completed over a dozen large projects, including transforming the old five-and-dime into the Kress Legal Center and Law Library, and converting the J.C. Penny building into the Family Law Courthouse for the Superior Courts of California.

I now travel and lecture at colleges passing on the lessons I've learned over the course of my career. In addition, when the mayor of Pacific Grove, California, a town of approximately 16,000 residents on the Monterey Peninsula, I partnered with the community to begin to create a green, self-sustaining environment. The hope is that this town will become a model for sustainable living.

Becoming a Contra-developer

I describe myself not as a developer but as a "contra-developer" because just about everything about the way I operate—my education, building philosophy, and methodology—is contrary to the standard operating procedures followed by most developers.

In the past several decades, these developers, enabled by city and county officials, have aggressively pursued sprawl development—building into rural areas that became first and second generation suburbs. They have paved over farmland and built new, expensive, and sterile construction, such as big-box stores and cookie-cutter housing, with little thought to the environmental repercussions or the more immediate costs of new infrastructure. Much of the expense of the new roads or the police and fire services required by these building booms has been borne by the taxpayers, not the developers, and will continue to be in the future.

One reason these developments have been more lucrative, and less restrained, is because they are not hampered by the regulations with which architectural preservationists must contend. But look at the consequences. Many of these developments, built with no eye to the future, have been deserted and more will be abandoned in the future. As fossil fuels and other resources become more limited, the expense of living far from a town center will become less practical. It's a lifestyle we can no longer support.

I advocate turning around the trend toward sprawl by enticing people back into city and town centers where they can live, work, be entertained, shop, and conduct business without having to drive thirty miles in one direction to get to the office and twenty miles in another to see a movie. Restoring existing city structures that already contain intact infrastructures and exemplify our architectural heritage is the first step toward saving ourselves.

We need to become re-involved with one another and our communities. In a sprawl environment, there's a tendency to retreat, to cocoon instead of congregate. Many people have forgotten the rewards of being an integral part of a community, sharing daily concerns with others. Individuals now live tethered to beeping electronic gadgets, constantly checking their Blackberry® smartphones for text messages and emails, a poor substitute for face-to-face interactions with fellow humans.

At the Crossroads

We are at a major crossroads in all of our institutions, many of which are dramatically failing. The depletion of our energy resources is going to force a change in lifestyle. One day soon, even developers and government agencies addicted to the quick buck and in denial of future consequences, will have to come to terms with the facts. The old way is not working anymore. We now have a president who understands the need for fresh ideas to meet the challenges of the future. This is encouraging.

Old Ferry Building is now a public market, Market Street, San Francisco.

What's needed is a paradigm shift, a turnaround—in perception about how we live; in government regulations and incentives; in community service; and in entrepreneurial ventures. Just as we are now paying the price for the bad decisions of the past, our children and grandchildren will be profoundly affected by our decisions and actions today. I believe that a completely different approach to the built environment is necessary to our survival.

Thanks to a plethora of buildings begging to be restored and adapted to new uses, there are many city, towns, and neighborhoods that are ideal candidates to be contra-developed. These buildings should not be languishing; they should be utilized. Here's why:

- Many have at least partially intact infrastructures.
- They were constructed with materials of a much higher quality than are used now.
- Seeing, feeling and touching historic architecture connects us to the past, and in turn motivates us to connect to the future.
- Older architecture displays the character and care absent from most modern developments.
- Restoration can drastically cut down on fossil fuel consumption.

Restoring and readapting historic architecture and putting it to good use is one of the greenest, most sustainable things we can do.

There are so many options, so many ways to make a positive impact if you think imaginatively. One building can be transformed into a live/work space. Another can be made to accommodate several tenants, including small businesses or non-profits that make a social contribution to the community. Another can be transformed into a ballet school. One renovation in a section of town can trigger others, and before you know it, a whole neighborhood is revitalized.

D*owntown Turnaround* combines story and information. The stories concern my professional development and some of the surprising, gratifying experiences I've had while restoring properties. The project chapters provide information on how each property was purchased, financed, renovated and completed. After reading this book, you will have a foundation of ideas, strategies, and examples to deal constructively with the challenges you face as you create your own restorations, renovations or contributions to your communities.

"The House of the Future" describes how I got started. "City Planning" analyzes how we got to where we are, and the importance of city planning. "Urban Building Blocks" introduces the urban building blocks that will be referred to throughout the book. It provides a synopsis of each piece in the renovation puzzle. The Urban Building Blocks are: Choosing a Project; Financing; Design Considerations; Finding Tenants; Public-Private Partnerships; and Regulations and Requirements. Subsequent chapters provide a project-by-project tour of a variety of renovations, each with a unique story. Using the building blocks as guides, the procedures for each property will be elucidated.

The specific challenges of each job will expose you to the many aspects of the trade. You'll have an overview of the processes and a variety of tools for solving the problems that can save our architectural heritage and improve the environment. You won't have all the answers–who does?–but you will know what questions to ask to re-enliven your town, city, or neighborhood on whatever scale you choose.

Create Your Fortune: Recognize Potential

Downtown Turnaround will help you understand the full potential of that abandoned schoolhouse. You'll know that in order to mine that potential, the most essential elements you need are imagination, willingness to think outside the box, enthusiasm, and the ability to find the right partners. You'll be able to envision the building's transformation from ugly, neglected, and bereft of tenants to a handsome, fully-utilized and occupied, economically viable entity. You'll have some ideas about how to find financing, even if you're starting with almost nothing. You'll know what kind of partners to seek. You'll have the satisfaction of seeing how your success will enhance a neighborhood, prompting more economic and community activity and positively affecting the lives of people in ways that will surprise you. You'll see your contribution to a sustainable green environment. You'll discover that this is an entrepreneurial venture that not only benefits your community, but can also prove to be very lucrative. You will see with new eyes.

I challenge you to make your fortune while making the world more green and sustainable. Look around your community, nearby city or town center. Find an abandoned building and join with others to transform it into something that benefits the community. Live in it, or create office space, a restaurant, a book store, a computer graphics business, a medical clinic. The possibilities are endless.

The House of the Future

"I have an affection for a great city. I feel safe in the neighborhood of man, and enjoy the sweet security of the streets."
Henry Wadsworth Longfellow

I love cities. I love the energy, the tempo, the variety of faces, places and experiences. A vibrant city is like an aromatic, mouth-watering feast spread across a candle-lit table laden with an array of cuisines, from the rarest delicacies and ethnic dishes to hot dogs and French fries. A great city has something for everyone—residential neighborhoods, business and commercial districts, entertainment, cultural institutions, schools, colleges, squares and parks. Streets and architecture reverberate with history and the countless stories of our forebears. A city has a rhythm, a buzz. It opens to the world inviting it in, and the world accepts the invitation. Brushing up against a crush of people as they hurry about their lives is a happy reminder that we're all in this together.

I grew up in the great city of San Francisco. From the Ferry Building on the bay to the Cliff House overlooking the Pacific, I came to know all its tantalizing neighborhoods, its physical beauty, its rich history expressed through its architecture, its diversified, intact communities, and its seamier side. Every city has its share of crime and homelessness, but that too is part of its identity.

And I learned how it functioned. In my teens, I did some basic carpentry work on Victorians in the Fillmore district—not the most appealing neighborhood in the city—and witnessed a transformation that made a big impression on me. In my early twenties, the seeds planted in childhood developed into a vocation: to preserve our beautiful, abandoned architectural heritage by renovating old buildings and reinvigorating the surrounding areas.

Vintage cable car at the new-use Ferry Building and downtown San Francisco, with Coit Tower in the distance.

Coming of Age

My coming of age was in the late 1960s and early 1970s. Like most young people, I did what I loved: played guitar and listened to music, spent a lot of time outdoors, learned to build houseboats, hosted a radio show. But I knew one thing when I left home for college: I was on my own, and would need to make a living eventually. It would take me a while to settle on how.

While in college at the University of the Pacific in Stockton, I was fortunate to meet Guard Darrah, a retired district attorney, from whom I rented a cabin. He also owned several acres and a small island on the Calaveras River, a tributary of the San Joaquin River, which would become the site of an experiment in sustainable living among some friends and myself. We were just trying to live independently, building our own living spaces and growing our own food. We were ahead of our time but didn't know it.

Darrah was a wonderful eccentric, which was evident in the unusual things he collected. If a building somewhere caught his fancy, he would buy it and bring it home, even if that meant mounting it on a barge and tugging it up the San Joaquin. He owned several structures from the 1939 San Francisco World's Fair, two of which I called home for a time. His personal residence had once been the Fair's House of Ireland. Darrah also had a penchant for collecting parts of old battleships and carting them home. The treasures were deposited in the the huge field behind his house.

It was truly an other-worldly time. I lived in a small cabin in a field surrounded by a sculptural jungle of ship parts, which cast eerie shadows under the moonlight. The cabin was one of Darrah's prizes, having been the dressing room for Sally Rand, a famous fan dancer. Later I moved from that dressing room to the big stage of the island, where other items in his collection had accumulated. Among them was the World Fair's House of the Future, a skeletal structure devoid of right angles and replete with roof holes and cracks. I had no idea how portentous the name of that building would prove to be.

Sustainable Living Experiment

So began my Robinson Crusoe phase. Could a city kid get the hang of country living? There was a lot to learn. Did you turn a chicken upside down and shake it to get eggs? What kind of food could I grow? After figuring out how to make a living space, how would I heat it? I had little money, so I had to be as self-sufficient as possible.

The island posed many construction challenges, but one of its big advantages was the lack of building codes. A group of friends and I learned the basics of renovation in an unregulated environment. Living along a major waterway was a terrific asset. We ran water and electrical lines from one end of the island to the other. We experimented with methane generation, grew our own vegetables, and recycled everything that we couldn't burn in our stove. Foliage guaranteed privacy, and the large old oak and acacia trees provided dead wood for our fireplaces. We insulated the interior of the House of the Future and constructed livable spaces using indigenous bamboo and other scavenged materials. A mural of spear-carrying African warriors emerged on the outer walls, courtesy of classmates in my college art workshop, providing a startling image to boaters on the Calaveras.

Mining the talents of artists is a tradition I've continued. Whenever possible, I incorporate artwork in my projects. It enlivens environments and feeds our souls, which have become deeply undernourished.

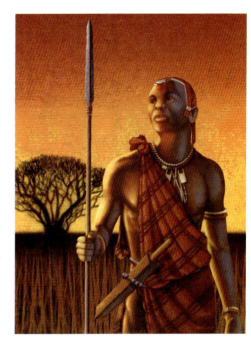

Warrior mural rendition courtesy Jupiter Images.

The lack of restriction and oversight allowed our little island group to experiment in ways we'd never get away with in a city. A houseboat was built in the shape of an elephant, and I built the first floating yurt, modeled on an Afghan A-frame tent. In his book, *How Buildings Learn*, Stewart Brand writes, "Projects flourish in the low-supervision environment." On Darrah's island, flourish we did.

The experience armed me with a certain fearlessness, a willingness to get my hands dirty, and the conviction that I could skillfully manage the roadblocks within the regulated environments of all my subsequent projects. I had learned by doing; I had made mistakes along the way, but this nitty-gritty, on-the-ground basic training provided a set of tools that many developers and architectural preservationists lack. It's great to be able to think conceptually and theorize, but the real learning comes from doing the work and finding solutions for the unique problems presented by individual projects.

Reentering Mainstream America

Of course, all good things must come to an end, and so it was with my Crusoe experiment. After about three years, I was ready to live and work in town again. I had not lost my love of cities and reentered Stockton's downtown with a renewed sense of purpose. Unlike in San Francisco, where prices were out of sight, in Stockton I could attempt, little by little, to revitalize a once-thriving city center full of historic architecture.

I was working toward my master's degree in education, teaching at a private inner city Catholic school and renovating Victorians part time. Eventually, I started my own business devoted to historic renovations, and now the subjects of my teaching are preservation and sustainability.

My first venture into renovation was the purchase of a small Victorian. I sold my old Ford Fairlane and my stereo to come up with the $2,000 down payment. Next, I got some friends and neighbors to invest. There was a carpenter who wanted to be a contractor one day and needed practice. Other individuals participated to hone specific skills. I'd learned that to be successful on a project one had to form partnerships that were mutually beneficial and that would get results.

Later when I needed a loan for a second Victorian, I went to the Bank of Stockton. The long-time president, Bob Eberhardt, whose grandfather had founded the bank and whose father was the previous president, was also a University of the Pacific grad. One day I stopped in at the bank and talked with him about sports and swimming—we had both been on the swim team—until he finally asked why I was there. I said I needed $10,000 to buy an old Victorian in a neighborhood he may have lived in as a kid. His reply was, "Sure, I'll do it for you, kid."

When he called in the loan executive, his words were: "Sign him up; I think he'll pay us back." It was possible to do business like that in those days.

For some reason, Bob believed in me, even though my track record consisted of a single Victorian. He trusted I would make good on the loan, and I did. Even more important, he believed in my vision of community and my intention to preserve the architectural heritage of his hometown. I was able to persuade him that my projects supported the lifestyles and small businesses of people living within the community, which was in sharp contrast to the sprawl and big-box store development his bank supported at the time.

Bob's support was crucial to my success. I could always count on him to consider the project that I was working on respectfully, and then make the loan.

A Contra-developer's Beginnings

It was probably around this time that I realized I was a contra-developer, that what I considered to be a positive approach to development was contrary to the philosophy and practice of others in the field. My interest was not in building new structures, but in preserving existing ones, and in so doing retaining our neglected architectural heritage. Observing the exodus from cities to newly developed suburbs, I foresaw the deterioration of our city centers and its negative effects on our economy and environment. I worked hard in Stockton to offset some of the worst effects of the movement.

As a self-taught contra-developer, I discovered my own solutions to the challenges of restoration and renovation. Admittedly, many of my innovative tactics were necessitated by the need to keep a ravenous wolf from the door. (Contra-developers operate without a net so we have to be agile, quick, and flexible.) The wolf would appear in the guise of city inspectors arriving on a site a little earlier than expected, authorities on historic preservation and government officials imposing inappropriate regulations, painters and carpenters needing their paychecks *now*, and completed but empty units needing tenants *yesterday*. The wolf had to be fed and I had to think fast and make decisions in an instant to find the food to quell his hunger.

Once I was in the process of putting the last touches on a restaurant. I had assured the tenant he could take occupancy in two days (otherwise he'd have to pay another month's rent where he was). I wanted him in so that I could pay the mortgage. Things seemed to be going along fine. We were just about finished with the renovation when the city inspector came and okayed the project. In the afternoon another city inspector arrived and overrode the first inspector's approval because he thought the fire protection rating for the ceiling tiles was unacceptable. Specific amounts of time are allocated for ceiling tiles to retard flames depending on the situation; for example, sometimes the requirement is twenty minutes; sometimes it's an hour. In this case, the first inspector had approved the lower amount of time, but the second insisted on what's called "one-hour fire." This difference of opinion between the two inspectors meant all the panels and cabling had to be changed. We worked straight for two days and redid the ceilings at a much-increased cost, but the tenant was able to move in on time, and I was able to make a mortgage payment to the bank.

These are the kinds of obstacles that come up all the time in restoration projects, and they are due, in part, to a misunderstanding about the differences between historic properties and newly built ones. It's an important distinction and one I'll be addressing in greater detail as the book progresses.

I still direct my company and properties in Stockton while living in Pacific Grove. Each challenge I face is a teacher, and the lessons I've learned throughout my working life are described in the following chapters. I hope they give you a headstart so that you can apply your energies toward turning around the destructive trend of the past decades and creating a healthier future for everyone.

City Planning

"Working adults formerly enjoyed an hour of 'community time' after the workday was over and before they were expected home. It has been replaced by an hour of 'commuting time.' The former warmed us to our fellow human beings, the latter conditions us to hate them."

Ray Oldenburg, *Celebrating the Third Place*

What Happened?

Ten years ago, I was invited to speak at the Frank Lloyd Wright School of Architecture in Arizona. Two women sitting near the stage of the large amphitheatre had a lot of questions. They were passionate to the point where, finally, both stood up. One had tears in her eyes, while the other asked, "What do we do? We used to have a neighborhood. We don't have a neighborhood anymore. We have a residential environment with a Blockbuster Video on one end and a Taco Bell on the other where there used to be a nice little café and bookstore. Now we're just a thoroughfare, and they drive through our neighborhood fast and children are in jeopardy. What happened?"

This woman was articulating the alienation from their communities so many Americans feel today.

This chapter will address the questions in the minds of many Americans. Why are so many of our once-thriving cities deteriorating to such a level that no one wants to live in them anymore? Why have developers and city planners persisted in building in rural areas, paving over valuable farmland, erecting housing developments and big-box retail stores, and creating new infrastructures, when they could have been investing in the cities with intact infrastructures? Why have so many small businesses gone under? Why are so many people feeling isolated and cut off from community?

The answer to all those questions is the same: poor planning by developers, bankers, mortgage companies, and politicians motivated by self-interest, rather than the long-term quality of life for the public. Yes, people were seeking different lifestyles in the suburbs, but had the difficult aspects of city life been approached with an eye toward saving them rather than abandoning them, we would be in a much better situation today.

Victorian, downtown Pacific Grove.

City Planning Basics: An Overview

Good city planning can provide powerful tools for positive change, but radical changes are called for on all levels: in perception about the way we live, in government regulations, in building practices, in community action, and in entrepreneurial ventures. There is great opportunity now to restore and renovate bringing downtown areas back to health, while making a profit. For constructive change to take place, however, everyone concerned has to become active in the solution. The old slogan from the sixties stands: "If you're not part of the solution, you're part of the problem."

The structure of planning departments varies depending on whether the city is a general law or a charter city. A general law city is managed by a five-member elected city council. A charter city defines its governing system by its own charter rather than by state, provincial, regional or national laws. A charter city can adapt or modify its charter by a majority vote of residents. In California, the majority of cities are charter cities.

Pacific Grove, for example, is a charter city. The city council hires and fires city managers and attorneys, who hire and fire everyone else—police, fire, public works, community development. The city council and the mayor make policy, working with residents to create a general plan of what they want their city to look like, then deliver it to the planning department which carries it out. A general plan is effective for ten years, at which time it's reviewed and, if desired, revamped.

Remodeled Victorian in the Magnolia District, Stockton.

Money and the Quick Fix: Tax Revenues

Why does bad planning happen, especially when citizens are not involved? Where to start? Money, of course. Big-box stores and other developments bring tax revenues to cities, and cities need that money. They need it for services, maintenance, improvements, new projects, their salaries, and employee salaries. Add to this the short-sightedness of politicians with limited terms, the poor hands-on training of some city planners and architectural preservationists, and the lack of participation from citizens, and you have the perfect soil for big-box stores with big tax revenues to take root outside city centers. This, in turn, reduces or eliminates commerce for small and/or minority-owned businesses, usually forcing them out of an area, and thus precipitating their decline.

The people making the decisions are saying, "We would rather have a lot of money coming in right now than think about the repercussions of our decisions in fifteen years when we'll be out of office." Meanwhile, all their employees at the government level are being paid by the tax revenues brought in by those big-box stores. In short, tax revenue pays for government.

What's not being taken into account when building out and creating more sprawl are the hidden costs to government that are passed on to taxpayers for the necessary additional infrastructure. These include roads, sewers, salaries, equipment, facilities for firefighters, police, and other services to accommodate the outlying areas. As we respond to the environmental crisis, this is proving to be even more of a problem. However, if these development assumptions remain unchallenged, city officials will continue to allow what is more immediately lucrative at the expense of what is necessary for responsible growth and a sustainable environment.

Past and Future Cities

Given the pressing environmental and economic challenges we face, what are the characteristics of an ideal city or town? My response is simple: *The cities of the past are the cities of the future.*

I'm not talking about

Lighthouse Avenue, downtown Pacific Grove.

the return of the horse and buggy, gas lamps, child labor, or unsafe working and living conditions. What I am advocating for is returning populations to centralized areas where one doesn't need to drive miles to get to work, shop, see a doctor, consult a lawyer, or go to a movie. I'm also advocating for returning to the values of caring about our neighbors and communities, respecting history and our architectural heritage, and husbanding our natural resources.

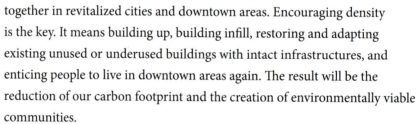

Below and facing page: Lighthouse Avenue, Pacific Grove.

Elements of Good City Planning

In the 21st century, good city planning requires thinking about the future in an intelligent, informed way. It implies a knowledge of building and architecture, of history, of a community and the desires and needs of its residents.

The basic elements that comprise the best city and urban village environments are listed below.

❒ Community Participation and Involvement

Public participation is the single most important factor for good city planning. When people who actually live in a community take responsibility for providing input, then the most change will occur. Otherwise, cities will continue going for the quick fix. If you want good economic growth and a sustainable environment, you need to speak up. Go to meetings, get to know your elected officials, let them get to know you and your concerns, organize with people of like mind, and lobby for changes in outdated or unnecessary regulations. Patronize and protect small businesses in your area. Get a growers' market going in your town once a week to support local farmers. Keep yourself informed about the decisions being made in the city planning offices. Participate.

❒ Compact, efficient land use—building up, not out

Density is not a four-letter word. Conserving land and energy means, in practical terms, living closer

together in revitalized cities and downtown areas. Encouraging density is the key. It means building up, building infill, restoring and adapting existing unused or underused buildings with intact infrastructures, and enticing people to live in downtown areas again. The result will be the reduction of our carbon footprint and the creation of environmentally viable communities.

Thanks to an abundance of land, Americans haven't had to learn the lessons of efficient land use that Europeans and Asians have been practicing for years. Americans must learn to appreciate, not only the efficiency that comes with density, but also the economic and intellectual stimulation. Cities with large populations of residents and visitors have energy that can be harnessed and used collaboratively and creatively. When you think of an exciting, vibrant city, which one comes to mind? New York? Charlottesville? Amsterdam? Rome? Paris? London? Buenos Aires? The best cities are crowded; that is, dense, with people bumping up against each other.

San Francisco is densely populated and has all the attributes of a great city. It also has crime, several big-box stores and chains, and its share

The Old Bath House, a Pacific Grove destination for decades, is being renovated as a new, sustainable seafood restaurant.

of homeless people. But it has not fallen victim to sprawl the way so many other cities have; one reason is that it's built on a seven-mile long peninsula and there's nowhere else to go. This unyielding space limitation forces solutions to problems that don't include building out, but do include infill and building up. Space is not wasted.

The same is true of my town of Pacific Grove, a small city quite different from San Francisco, but the space constriction is also present. It's only two-and-a-half miles long and there's no more land on which to build. We could do some infill, we could build a second floor here and there, we could reutilize buildings for new purposes, but we're not going to build two hundred housing units because we don't have the land to do it. This, to my mind, is a blessing. The challenge is to constrain growth when there are no physical limitations.

❐ Restoration and Preservation

It's a waste of resources to build new structures when there are so many buildings with intact infrastructures that can be restored at a much lower cost. Adaptive re-use; that is, transforming an old building to meet present-day needs, is the most energizing form of downtown revitalization. This approach demands a change in perception by most city planners and developers. Changing the perception is central to my work as a contra-developer and one of my motivations for writing this book.

❐ Sustainable Economies with Support to Small Businesses

Central to good city planning is the idea of supporting small, local businesses. In addition to discouraging the building of big-box stores, supporting small businesses means buying from them, even if it costs a little more. As a contra-developer, I often give small businesses the opportunity to incubate in my properties. I may offer lower rent for the first years while a business gets on its feet and then bring the rate up to market level. We need to support the local café, bookstore, and computer repair shop if people are going to claim ownership in a community and make it a desirable place to live.

❐ Enlivened Self-Sustaining Cities and Downtowns

Healthy communities, in which people care about each other and their environments, are key to enlivening our cities and towns. Recreating community in our downtowns and city centers means

Monday Farmers Market on Lighthouse Avenue, downtown Pacific Grove.

creating mixed-use environments with buildings and areas that contain residential, commercial, and public spaces. These are sometimes referred to as urban villages. Walking, biking and public transit must be encouraged and automobile traffic discouraged. This works when shopping and service facilities are centralized. Returning to wider sidewalks with more room for street and social activity and less room for speeding cars will add to a more manageable, less frenetic lifestyle. In addition, city centers and downtowns should include public meeting places and centers for gatherings, discussions, performances, and other group activities. Living, working, and socializing in the same city/town creates a healthy social structure in which people are committed to maintaining and contributing to a community.

Summary

The elements described above must be conceived, born, and bred within city planning departments with input and strong support from those most affected by a city's decisions: its residents. We cannot depend on the government to take care of us, or some amorphous *other* with our best interests at heart. They do not exist, and it's time that everyone took part in creating a new world—one that is viable within our current constraints. If there is nothing stopping an entity from proceeding along a selfish, greedy track, there's no reason to stop doing so. Make your voice heard, and co-create the world you want to live in.

Urban Building Blocks

"The world will not evolve past its current state of crisis by using the same thinking that created the situation. "
Albert Einstein

Most developers buy land, get entitlements to build X amount of square footage with X amount of water and X amount of parking. They use a formula and a prescribed, progressive system of buying and building. They are supported by politicians and city planners because in the short term it may make sense and it will make money.

Contra-developers like myself start out with an entirely different set of assumptions and expected outcomes. I begin by locating buildings that no one wants in areas where no one wants to be, and find ways to have them given to me or purchase them at very low prices. I then locate financing and tenants in an attempt to create a higher quality environment for people.

All these projects have unique challenges, but each falls under a certain category, or rubric. I call them urban building blocks. Successful management of each will ultimately define your success. The basic building blocks of any successful restoration project are: Choosing a Project; Financing; Design Considerations; Finding Tenants; Public/Private Partnerships; and Regulations and Requirements. In real time and with real projects, they overlap and intertwine. For example, finding tenants influences the way a project is financed, and design considerations are affected by municipal and state regulations as well as the potential tenant mix.

Please understand that this chapter will not explicate every circumstance that could occur, nor every resource there is for historic development—there will be no charts, graphs, or statistics. However, the information here will provide a general foundation, including several specific items of information and suggestions, from which you can conduct your own research to fit your particular situation. The project chapters will offer more detail regarding solutions necessitated by the specific challenges of each building block for the individual properties.

Show and Tell

Although this is not a building block, I include a brief explanation of my show–and–tell philosophy, because in my experience nothing else works as well in the right circumstances.

If one simply talks about or describes a concept that's a little out of the ordinary or involves a new or different approach to any of the building blocks, very few people are able to visualize the description. For example, the concept of the urban village, which you will be reading about, was not grasped in Stockton until after we completed the Eden Square project. Then and only then was the idea understood. Time after time I've demonstrated that something can work in spite of naysayers and individuals who refuse to use their imaginations, but I've had to be a pioneer breaking new ground.

From restoring the building that no one else wants in a neglected neighborhood to inspiring investment from developers and citizens into that same community, a contra-developer is always fighting the status quo. Show and tell can sometimes be quite an undertaking, but if you believe in what you're doing and have done your homework, don't let yourself be stopped by those who are stuck in the way things have always been. Show them another way.

SIX URBAN BUILDING BLOCKS

- ❏ Choosing a Project
- ❏ Financing
- ❏ Design Considerations
- ❏ Finding Tenants
- ❏ Public/Private Partnerships
- ❏ Regulations and Requirements

Above: Cort Tower was placed on the National Historic Register in 1980. Courtesy the Bank of Stockton Historical Photograph Collection. Below: West End, Sand City

Above: Heritage Square building, Stockton. Right: Eden Square building, Stockton. Below: Railroad Square building, Historic Landmark No. 41 designated by Stockton City Council in 1986. Courtesy the Bank of Stockton Historical Photograph Collection.

Choosing a Property

We all have specific needs, ideas, or visions that shape our choices. My initial choices were Victorian homes in a particular Stockton neighborhood. I wanted to restore, renovate, and sometimes repurpose by, for example, transforming living rooms and bedrooms into office space. These homes were in an area of Stockton that needed revitalization and were relatively small projects. When I was ready, I moved on to large commercial buildings, and then even larger ones.

You may only restore one building in a lifetime for your family to live in or for a small business you start, or, better yet, for both as owner/occupant. You may be one of many partners making a decision about investing in a property or part of a team that wants to bring several businesses together under one roof. You may be the director of a social service agency that needs more space. You may even be an architect, developer, city planner, or professional in sustainable urban growth who will take on many projects over your career.

As a contra-developer, I always go beyond bricks and mortar and consider the larger picture. I choose properties that will become *significant identifiers*; that is, projects that serve as impressive, visible examples of transformation in places that surprise people, including investors and developers. These serve as inspiration for others to invest in the reutilization of existing structures with the goal of recreating community.

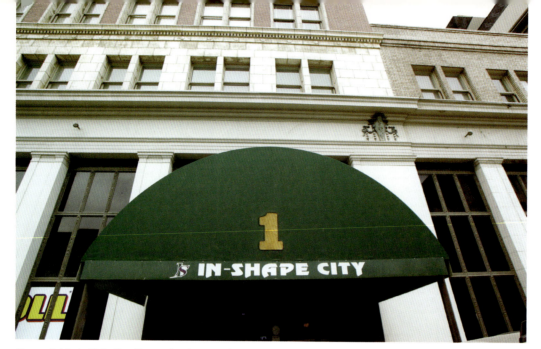

Above: Athletic Club, Cort Tower, Stockton. Right: Women's Center, Heritage Square, Stockton.

I ask specific questions about each structure. How will my work on this property affect and assist the community? How can I build in a way that benefits the environment as much as possible? What structures are already in the vicinity? What are the city and state regulations for preserving a historic building? What kinds of renovations will be needed to satisfy seismic retrofitting requirements or accommodations for the disabled? (These need to be included in the projected costs.) What is the zoning? Is it in an enterprise zone eligible for funding for specific types of building projects? What are the kinds of businesses or institutions that would be appropriate for the neighborhood, even if the business owners and institution officials haven't figured it out yet?

Often the building will tell you something about the way it should be used. This is not to say that when restoring a property it needs to be brought back to its previous incarnations; in fact, usually that's not the case. An old warehouse becomes a social service urban village containing several agencies under one roof, or an office building becomes a law library and legal center, or a convent is transformed into the headquarters for a woman's community center.

When you have gathered as much information as possible and consulted other professionals about the property and the surrounding area, it's time to calculate the cost of improvements, think about the future profitability of the purchase, and, of course, plan the financing. This is the time to consult your team or other partners, and most importantly to confer with an accountant who specializes in real estate. A long-term financial plan must be established. If you are satisfied that you can afford the property, repay loans, meet the regulations, make it profitable, and benefit the community, then sign on the dotted line.

Keep in mind that owning real estate provides numerous, substantial benefits that will add to the bottom line over time. These include depreciation, write-offs, tax benefits, and appreciation. Your accountant will provide the necessary expertise regarding those intangible advantages that are not obvious at the moment of sale, but will provide substantial assets in the future.

❐ Designation of a Historic Building

Renovation projects by definition almost always involve buildings with historic value. Definitions of "historic" vary, but if a structure is officially designated as "historic," or if it's situated in a historic district, every aspect of the project will be affected.

In California, the California Environmental Quality Act (CEQA) maintains that a study should be done on any building over fifty years old. The results of these studies can be enlightening. Not every building over fifty years old is necessarily one that should be preserved. Discernment is required.

The National Trust for Historic Preservation's definition of an historic building is that someone important lived or worked there, or that the building has good architecture. To my mind, an historic building is one that both the community and the developer agree possesses the attributes of good architecture, historical identity, and utility. Although they are not strictly historical considerations, I must, as a contra-developer, take into account affordability and large open spaces that can be readapted.

An advantage to restoring those historic buildings made with good materials and fine workmanship is that they're usually sturdy. It's a bonus if the infrastructure, such as plumbing, doesn't need to be upgraded or redone entirely. Some old buildings have been neglected for so long that the damage renders them not worth saving—at least not as viable structures that people can actually use and that can contribute to revitalization. Sometimes removing rather than restoring a structure is the best economic solution that will contribute to the commercial or residential health of an area. A new building in its place may be just what the area needs and may actually add to, not detract from, the historic fabric of a community.

Some modern architecture looks altogether appropriate next to older buildings. The juxtaposition of old and new—if the new isn't just a box—can be handsome and utilitarian while building a kind of architectural bridge between the past and present that suggests a healthy trend for the future. It's all about balance and how the architecture will serve the community.

Examples on both pages of architectural harmony with old and new buildings in downtown Stockton.

Urban Building Blocks 41

❐ Good Bones

I always make sure my properties have good bones. There are two kinds of "bones." The first is physical infrastructure, such as the soundness of support beams or the integrity of the roof.

I solicit engineering surveys on the quality of the infrastructure. Is there enough water and sewer capacity? Are the storm drains there? What's the state of the electrical system, the sprinkler system, the heating and air conditioning units, the elevators? I always make many visits to a prospective property. I find out its history and its past functions; that is, what went on architecturally before now? What were this building's incarnations? What was there before the façade was put on? Or if a façade is there, how can I save it? Many cities have loans to help refurbish the exterior of a building. Exteriors are significant; they sell the building.

The second kind of "bones" relates to the area itself. I find out if there's a city plan for that area, and, if so, if the plan is being followed and if my ideas are a good fit. If there's a degree of blight, homelessness, or crime, I consult with the city redevelopment office. Is it in an enterprise zone or a national historic district? Is other restoration or building intended for that neighborhood? The parking situation is also key. Is the renovation in a parking district or will I have to develop my own parking? Is there public transportation nearby? What are the municipal codes that must be adhered to?

I look for neighborhoods or districts with vitality, where I expect other buildings to be restored (such as an old downtown) or where there's already some interest in revitalization. Such neighborhoods support my vision, and help convince city officials it's a good investment. If I like a building, and the city doesn't have a vision for the area, then my vision must be even stronger.

Facing page: Early downtown Stockton. Courtesy the Bank of Stockton Historical Photograph Collection.

Right: Railroad Square, Stockton

❐ Architectural Styles and Economies of Scale

Each architectural style, whether it's Victorian, Romanesque, art deco, or beaux-arts, offers benefits and challenges. Becoming familiar with them is imperative. One of my objectives is to enhance the design elements that distinguish a building and give it character. I find ways to do this inside and out, so that, although an interior is all new and can be very modern, there are still indications of its history incorporated into the new design. For example, although an old warehouse is transformed into a social services center, the cylindrical ducts are visible and painted, and exposed brick walls and wide entrances maintain some of the old character.

Another thing to consider is economy of scale. Generally speaking, I like to get as big a property for as little as I can. Most people (especially government tenants) want more open space, because large spaces can always be made smaller. The opposite involves engineering, and that's expensive. Big spaces are safer bets. There's less to do.

Urban Building Blocks   43

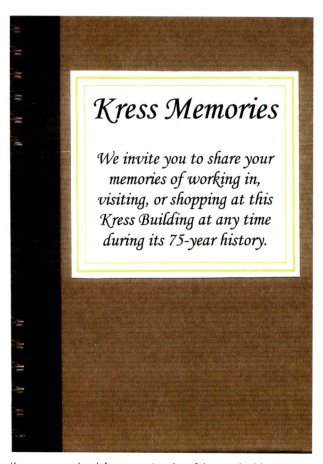

Kress memory book from opening day of the new building.

"The site I landed on [chose] feels much more isolated than it really is; it's almost magical. Within its limited radius, there was a whole range of the local ecology."

Martin Puryear

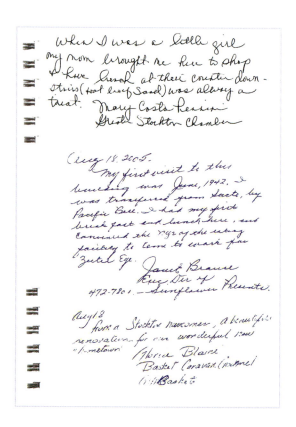

❐ Story Power and Magical Moments

Familiarity with an area is a great asset. I was able to do what I did in Stockton because it was my home for many years. I was part of the community and knew the business owners, county offices, and history of the town. I knew that certain places pulled on the heartstrings of people who once lived there, such as the Kress Building, which had been the local five-and-dime for decades and housed a popular soda fountain. Imagine the conversations that took place at that fountain over the years. Memories reverberate within that building, and they add to the richness of the space. Find people who have such recollections and listen to their tales. You will incorporate them into your story of the property that you pass on to prospective tenants and partners.

44 DOWNTOWN TURNAROUND • Lessons for a New Urban Landscape

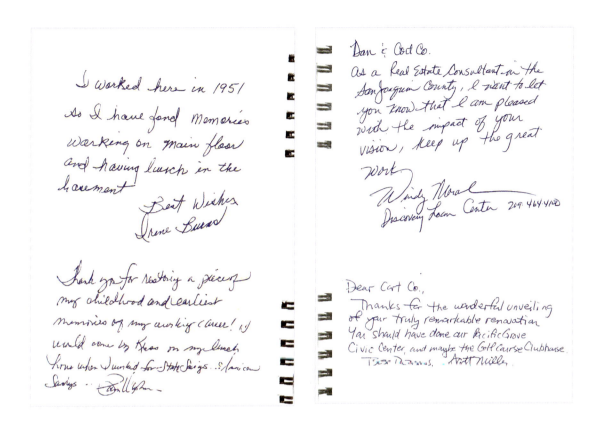

The power of storytelling is immeasurable and absolutely necessary to the goals of contra-developers. I would venture to say that it may be the thing that most distinguishes them from conventional developers. For a builder who simply wants to raze an area and build new, the story has no purpose.

Among the many joys and rewards of this profession are the unforeseen, serendipitous moments that appear like magic. These occur often, and I take them as messages that I'm doing what I should be doing. An energy is set in motion when you take on a project with a certain attitude, and then anything can happen. A person who saved your life may appear out of nowhere to rent a space, or you may find in a building a hidden treasure no one knew existed. A forty-five-year-old newspaper might fall into your arms providing just the communication you need. When these incidents occur, and they will, recognize and appreciate them. They're all part of the larger picture.

Although planning ahead for every circumstance isn't possible, being prepared is. Once you are, take on the project with optimism and vigor, trusting that there will be a solution for whatever unforeseen challenges arise.

Financing the Project

Contra-developers seek money for projects that are by their very nature viewed as a risk by big lending institutions and investors. Because you are proposing to bring a property from non-investment grade to investment grade, many lenders will not share your confidence that the property's value on completion will justify the investment you are asking them to make. That's why with financing, as with all the building blocks of contra-development, creativity is essential.

This is a challenging time to find money for real estate projects, just as it was for me in the seventies. However, there are still many resources and opportunities, especially for nontraditional projects that will eventually bring in surprisingly high profits. Seek out partners with imagination early on, people who trust that you can create a profitable property and who are happy to invest money or expertise. And don't forget show-and-tell! Show your past success–or, if you are new at it, show them what this book has taught you about how to succeed.

How does one get the money to realize a vision for a restoration whose value is not obvious to most people? Most of the time funds are derived from a variety of sources and at different times in the process. Financing a project can be a long-term proposition; some rewards are provided up front, but it takes a few years to realize the full and significant benefits of your investment. This section will present an overview of options and resources with which you should become familiar. Once you have gathered the necessary information and considered all the building blocks, then there are several alternative ways to piece together a good plan.

❏ Financial Advantages, Short and Long Term

There is a multitude of benefits when investing in real estate even if it is not a designated historic property, and even more when it is. Some of the returns on an initial real estate investment are not immediately tangible, but will be significant in the first year and will continue in subsequent years. Closing costs and interest payments are tax deductible. Then there's depreciation. The IRS assumes buildings (not land) depreciate over time, which translates into lower taxes. In fact, this is only an IRS distinction—more often, the building is actually appreciating in value with time, which is an advantage. With a fully amortized loan, every month a little principal is paid off and the mortgage is reduced, which

540 East Main Street, Stockton. Courtesy the Bank of Stockton Historical Photograph Collection.

has the effect of providing more equity on the property because principal is not taxed. In addition, certain improvements can also be written off. All these benefits come with most real estate purchases. Land alone cannot be depreciated.

Financing historic restoration has unique challenges and benefits. Because of the depressed nature of the properties involved, contra-developers spend much less on the initial property purchase than other developers. There are also financial breaks for these projects through, among other things, the Mills Act, a 1972 California law specifically marked for historic preservation projects that allows cities to enter into contracts with the owners of historic structures. Such contracts require a reduction of property taxes in exchange for the continued preservation of the property. Property taxes are recalculated using a formula in the Mills Act and Revenue and Taxation Code.

Building in a designated enterprise zone—areas of blight targeted to encourage restoration—can also provide great benefits, including tax credits for employees and rapid depreciation on equipment. If the property you're renovating is a national historic landmark, or if you have it designated as such, there are other benefits. These often come with strings attached, but usually the financial advantage is worth the price you pay in aggravation. Over the years, for example, there are significant savings in income taxes through rapid depreciation of the building.

Another benefit to be aware of is that when selling a building, if purchasing another property or exchanging from one to another, it's possible to defer the gain through an IRS 1031 tax-deferred exchange, which could result in as much as a 20 percent or more savings on the sale. (See 540 East Main Street.)

Urban Building Blocks   47

❐ Loans

Big banks are not particularly receptive to the contra-developer's goals, so better resources are community banks and investment groups. For many years my primary lender was the Bank of Stockton, because the president believed in my vision, even while his bank promoted big-box developers. My relationship with the bank changed after he died, and I started borrowing from other small institutions. To acquire the necessary support from a bank, its officials have to be convinced that your project will be valuable and profitable to a community the bank wants to see thrive. It's the developer's job to persuade them of its worth.

❐ Investors

Investments come in the form of money or time and services. Financial investors may be family, friends, associates, or people familiar with your community who want to see it improved. Just as there are tax advantages for the new owner of a property, there are similar tax benefits for investors. A variety of positive arrangements can be worked out with investment partners.

A contribution of time, talent, or labor is another kind of investment. For example, a contractor may offer free labor on a project with the condition that he or she may occupy a residence, business, or office rent-free for a specified period of time upon completion.

The more information you have about financing sources, the better equipped you'll be to create an efficient plan. Money is needed to cover both the purchase price and tenant improvements, which are usually substantial. These costs must be factored into the plan and the appropriate loans found. Your preliminary investigation will inform decisions in every step of the process, even ones for which you hadn't planned. When an unforeseen circumstance occurs (and it will, especially if you're involved in several projects), draw on your knowledge and creativity to craft innovative financing solutions.

Historic restorations are eligible for many grants and loans through government on city, county, state, and federal levels. I mentioned the Mills Act and enterprise zones. Investigate these resources in the city development or redevelopment offices, which can guide you to sources such as the federal Community Reinvestment Act (CRA), Community Development Block Grants (CDBG), façade grants, and others. The National Trust for Historic Preservation and, in California, SHPO (State Historic Preservation Officer), have extensive information, as well as educational and technical assistance.

Other resources include low-interest community reinvestment monies available from local or community banks, and Small Business Association loans. Find the kind of support that works for you, while being discriminating about the costs to your project.

California Historical Property/Mills Act

The Mills Act is an economic incentive program in California for the restoration and preservation of qualified historic buildings by private property owners. Enacted in 1972, the Mills Act legislation grants participating local governments (cities and counties) the authority to enter into contracts with owners of qualified historic properties who actively participate in the rehabilitation, restoration, preservation, and maintenance of their historic properties. Since the costs of doing so can be prohibitive, property tax relief can offset these costs.

In 1976, California voters passed Proposition 7, amending Section 8 of Article XIII of the California Constitution requiring enforceably restricted historical properties be valued on a basis that is consistent with its restrictions and uses. Sections 439 through 439.4 of the Revenue and Taxation Code set forth the statutory authority for the assessment of Mills Act properties. Essentially, it provides that valuation of the property be determined by the income approach rather than a sales data approach, even for an owner-occupied single-family residence.

Mills Act contracts are for an initial term of 10 years. A contract automatically renews each year on its anniversary date and a new 10-year agreement becomes effective, creating a "rolling" contract term that is always equal to the initial contract term.

If you still have questions, you may call the State Board of Equalization at 916 445 4982. You may also contact your local governmental agency that administers the program in your city or county. Source:

www.boe.ca.gov/proptaxes/faqs/faqs_mills_act.htm

❐ Innovation

Innovative financing arrangements can be negotiated that work for all parties. For example, I made a deal with one owner (Railroad Square) to pay nothing to buy the building, with the understanding that when the project started to bring in money, he would earn more than his asking price.

There are all sorts of possible creative and viable transactions that can work in a given situation. Don't be afraid to make an offer if you think it will work, no matter how new or radical it may appear to be. The important thing is to make it work.

❐ Leases

Along with renovations costs, projected rental rates are included in the financing plan and can be shaped to work for you and the tenant. For example, one can make an agreement with tenants that for a set amount of time they will be charged lower-than-market rates and after that time, escalators will be built into the lease to bring them to market rates. Knowing who your tenants are ahead of time is a great help. Government agencies are particularly good, dependable tenants. You'll read about a variety of innovative rental arrangements in the following chapters.

7th Street Tenants-in-Common, Pacific Grove.

Design Considerations

The construction phase is the culmination of all the previous work and planning for a project. The re-adaptation and redesign of a property may be the most exciting tasks. This is the puzzle piece in which the vision, the physical plan devised at the beginning of the project, is realized. Contractors are busy tearing down walls and rebuilding staircases, installing electrical, air conditioning, heating, sprinkler, and other necessary systems. Space is opened up and re-formed. The exterior is transformed from a beaten, neglected façade to a handsome, inviting one. Unusual and surprising events often occur during this phase. The ones you don't foresee are challenging and fun because they compel innovative solutions.

The initial steps go all the way back to before the purchase of the property, when the adaptive design begins to form in the mind. Design follows function and the requirements of the individuals, businesses, or agencies we perceive as our future tenants. A law library will have different structural needs from a daycare center or a ballet school. If it's a multi-use facility, you will be building for several entities under one structure, and each will demand its own design solutions.

As I toss out ideas, my architect apprises me of whether or not they're practical or even possible and how they might be carried out. Sometimes renderings of these ideas are shown to prospective tenants. If they decide to rent, the design becomes a plan. Eventually, a general, overall design is agreed upon based on the lessees we expect to occupy space. Sometimes we wait on large areas until we're actually in construction, and a tenant comes to us with a specific need. There is always the understanding that design modifications will need to be made in response to unforeseen circumstances. It's a fluid process, and the first space we construct may be readapted down the road when a new occupant with different needs moves in.

San Joaquin County Law Library, Kress Building, Stockton.

❐ Challenges and Surprises

During the renovation phase, each property reveals its quirks and challenges. Since there are very few restrictions for construction on the interior of a designated historic building, it's an opportunity to be creative.

By the time you get to this stage, you and your architect have developed a sound plan for the major structural changes and you're aware of the various systems that need refurbishing or replacing. In addition, the plans have taken into account regulations that must be met, including accommodations for the disabled, seismic retrofitting, and other elements that will affect the design.

Often in the case of large, old buildings that have been through other renovations, the original building plans have disappeared. This signals the strong probability that the building contains hidden architectural features that are not apparent at the time of purchase or during visits to the property beforehand. Such discoveries can affect the design. The chapter on Cort Tower describes one of the most dramatic concealed treasures I've come across, and its discovery actually simplified our construction plan.

Finds like these are likely to occur in buildings that have been adapted several times. I usually welcome such an occurrence, because it reveals a new aspect of the property and is often easily incorporated into the design. It also adds to the building's story and mystery.

❏ Utility and Beauty

The building's original character is often preserved most noticeably on the façade. If not, a façade can be created that fulfills the same objective (see Railroad Square). With interiors, the integration of old and new can be very effective. For example, rough, exposed brick walls can encompass a cafeteria with modern furniture and amenities and look terrific.

The restrictions on construction for historic buildings mostly pertain to the exteriors. What a developer is allowed to do is usually limited to repairing, cleaning, and/or restoring the old façade. This is usually fine with me, as a good cleaning of brick and terra cotta exteriors, or a five-color paint job on a Victorian, can make a world of difference in presentation.

Cort Victorian renovations in the Magnolia District, Stockton.

❐ The Façade

They say you can't judge a book by its cover, but people usually do anyway. The same is often true with old buildings.

This is why I make every effort to attend to the façade as early in the process as possible. It's the first signal to the world that a transformation is taking place, that something new and alive is coming to the area. Changes are relatively simple (although expensive), since not many are allowed on the exteriors of historic structures. But they pack a powerful punch. The cleaning of the exterior and the addition of awnings and/or handsome lettering for large industrial buildings are messages that respectful, thoughtful attention is being paid to the property. Looks matter, so make your building look as good as possible as soon as possible.

Some old exteriors, like Stockton's beautiful Kress Building, are genuine representations of the era in which they were built. Restoring such a façade, with its art deco logo, its trademark yellow brick, and its terra cotta geometric patterns, produces a striking transformation. However, these simple improvements can be deceptively complicated and costly. One doesn't simply get a hose and wash down the façade, because some of the brick or terra cotta may be blown away. There are restrictions on which chemicals and materials can be used, and they come at a price. Specially trained technicians wearing protective equipment work on scaffolds to perform these restorations. In Stockton, special grants are available for building façades.

Examples in the project chapters will illustrate many of our approaches to design. Be aware that your final results will only be as good as the people you hire. These partners and your tenants are integral to a successful, profitable, re-enlivened property.

Athletic Club at Cort Tower, Stockton.

Finding Tenants

Every piece of the puzzle is important, but tenants are the magical piece, the seminal solution to the puzzle. From the moment I consider taking on a new property, I am already forming ideas of what the tenant mix will be. Sometimes I know exactly for whom I'm building. But there is also some truth to the "if-you-build-it-they-will-come" idea. This occurred several times when I recognized the potential for certain businesses and enlisted them in my renovation plans. These efforts included an aikido school, a law library, county offices, cafés, small businesses, and a health club. Having a vision is very important, but before going ahead, I make sure all aspects of a project have been considered as well as the needs of individuals and companies surrounding the property.

Other times it takes a while to bring in the perfect match, but there are always interim solutions while seeking that perfect tenant.

❏ Accommodating the Needs of Tenants

Tenants don't stay forever, but they will stay a very long time if treated well. That begins during the tenant improvement phase, when we create office space, classrooms, libraries, courtrooms, or living units that accommodate the needs of future occupants. This is one of the most appealing enticements to a prospective tenant. I will often approach a business, school, or government office that I know is looking for space (or having trouble meeting the rent), with an architectural rendering of what a space built specifically for them would look like.

Sometimes I'll go a step further and do something really unconventional. With the permission of the project negotiators, I will talk to individuals at all levels of the organization who will be utilizing the space. I'll interview them regarding how to accommodate their needs and create a pleasant working environment.

I often get more information than I need, but the real purpose of this exercise is more far reaching. It is about offering everyone involved a sense of ownership. This investment of time and attention up front, going that extra mile, has enormous long-term benefits. When tenants feel seen and considered and a part of something larger, they become your partners in a community and tend to stay a long time.

After going through this process, I propose financial benefits, such as lower rental rates than are available elsewhere. Affordable rates and being made part of the renovation process is usually a very inviting combination for prospective tenants.

As I mentioned, to recoup my investment over time, I sometimes negotiate a low initial rate for a tenant coming in. We build escalators into the lease that kick in over time. In a good economic climate, we include cost of living adjustments. In more precarious times, we build in increases of no less than 3 percent or more than 5 percent after a specific length of time. These gradual adjustments to market rates make it possible to offer custom-made units at a low rent for the first couple of years, allowing the tenant an opportunity to incubate his or her business or settle into a living space. Eventually

Cort Companies executive offices, Cort Tower, Stockton.

rents are sufficient to cover the real costs of the project. We are still competitive in the marketplace, and profits are made.

One always wants to create win/win situations. When tenants know you care about them and their success, they will respond in kind, and good relationships are formed. You never know what might happen down the road; someday one of your tenants may invest in or purchase your building. (See Heritage Square and Sand City chapters.) We are all partners.

❐ Anchor Tenants

Usually the first order of business is to recruit the anchor tenant, the one whose rent will cover your mortgage and loan payments as you renovate and into the future. It's best if this can be done before signing the final purchase agreement, but in the real world that's not always possible. It is possible, however, and important to have an idea about what kind of tenant would be most appropriate for your building. The next step is to create enticements that will attract ideal tenants.

When I bought Cort Tower, I wanted to be assured that an anchor tenant was in place from the start. To this end, part of the purchase agreement was that the sellers, American Savings and Loan, agreed to rent two floors for five years. They became the anchor tenant. My company offices took

56 DOWNTOWN TURNAROUND • Lessons for a New Urban Landscape

over the tenth floor, and then I quickly got a number of small businesses and a health club to fill the building. American's rental made it possible to incubate smaller enterprises and allow them to grow. Without the agreement with American, it would have been far more difficult to offer that opportunity.

In a stable economy, one can expect the building to be occupied within six months. In an unstable economy, it may take longer. For a contra-developer, this creates an opportunity: Negotiate a lower purchase price and better terms to compensate for the delay. Temporary solutions, such as interim tenants, may also be available.

❐ Interim to Permanent Tenancy

When you first purchase a building it is important to get tenants in as quickly as possible, even if renovations are in progress, in order to meet as many expenses as you can. If the perfect fit is not immediately available, there are interim arrangements that can benefit owner and tenants. Many seasonal businesses have short-term space needs. A special festival may need temporary headquarters, or a consulting business may be in town for a limited time. Perhaps a company involved in a lawsuit needs work/meeting space for their attorneys.

Missing an opportunity to rent short-term could cost you, so it's important to get the word out that there is space available. A short-term tenant may even grow into the space. There are all sorts of arrangements that can be cobbled together if one thinks creatively. It's much better to have the lights on and keep a building warm than to maintain a cold, dark, empty structure, even for a little while.

Cort Companies conference room, Cort Tower, Stockton.

❐ Government Tenants

Government agencies are often anchor tenants in my properties and may occupy an entire building. (When a government entity rents from a private company, essentially you've got a public/private partnership (PPP).) Railroad Square is filled with county social service agencies. They are desirable occupants because they can be depended on to pay the rent on time. County and state agencies are among my tenants. Get to know your city and county organizations and keep informed about where they occupy space. This knowledge will be valuable if you find a property you think is particularly appropriate for a group looking to move. Government likes large spaces and economies of scale. If you purchase a big building, it may appeal to a specific group. These days, with furloughs and layoffs, government is as sensitive to the bottom line as the private sector. If they can get more space for less money, they're very interested.

❐ Private Business Tenants

As much as we need to encourage public/private partnerships, we also need to nurture and support small to mid-size businesses rather than the big box stores and chains that litter our suburbs. That's why I buy local and encourage others to do the same. I also rent to small businesses and they are often good tenants, but there's definitely more risk involved. In these difficult economic times, many businesses, small and large, are collapsing, and when this happens, everybody loses. The tenant loses a business, the owner loses a tenant, the community loses a service, the city may lose sales tax, and the way is opened for more big box retail with available tax credits to enter the scene. This is why it's so necessary for everyone to support small businesses.

For a business like mine, the combination of small to midsize businesses and government occupants is the optimal grouping in a property, and many of my projects contain this mix. As you proceed in your enterprises, the tenant or tenant-mix that works best for your property will become clear.

CalWORKS Employment Center, Railroad Square, Stockton.

Stockton PPPs. Left: Kress Building. Right: 600 E. Main Street.

Public/Private Partnerships (PPPs)

For many years, I've believed that more collaboration between private and public sectors in restoring the built environment would greatly benefit both sides and the whole country. A public/private partnership (PPP) describes a government service or private business venture which is funded and operated through a partnership of government and one or more private sector companies.

Financing is one way the public and private sectors work together as partners. Another is when a government entity rents from a private company. These arrangements are often of great benefit to both sides, as will be explained later.

Now more than ever, in this time of economic stress, it's necessary for the government and private sectors to cooperate in restoring facilities to create more utilitarian, less costly homes, work spaces, and jobs for the many Americans at risk.

While government is in the process of redefining its relationship to the private sector as it attempts to deal with the economic crisis, it's been clear to the building professions for a long time that government lacks efficiency in many areas. In general, the private sector tends to be quicker and cheaper when it comes to new or restored construction.

My company has proven that it can build in less than a quarter of the time for a fraction of the cost and do it better than a government agency can do it for itself. We accomplished this for the San Joaquin Department of Health, and their tenancy has been a great asset to us, creating the mutually beneficial partnership we hope to see happen more often. As you read on, there will be several examples of properties that were built through a PPP and have worked extremely well for both parties.

There are also other subtle but equally important benefits. For example, more open communication between the two sectors allows for better understanding of the challenges each faces. When the county is not only aware of but affected by certain (read: excessive) government regulations with which historic preservationists must contend, the possibility of modifying those regulations becomes more likely. It will take effort and good faith from both sides to create highly effective partnerships.

In terms of my work on specific properties, a PPP can begin very early in the process, even before a purchase, if the government agency agrees to become a tenant in a property when it is restored.

The restoration of 540 East Main Street was designed to accommodate the Family Law Courthouse for the Superior Courts of California. I bought Railroad Square with the idea that it was a perfect location and setting for county agencies. It didn't take much to sell them on the idea, and now the entire building is filled with social services agencies. The Kress Building and 600 East Main Street are also examples of successful PPPs, and sources of pride to my team.

I highlight these partnerships because of their importance and the necessity to keep nurturing them. The project chapters will shed light on how we have achieved good working relationships with government entities and provide examples of how others might do the same.

Stockton PPPs. Above: 540 E. Main Street. Below: Railroad Square.

Holman's Department Store, now an antique collective, envisioned by the owner as a luxury hotel on the Monterey Peninsula.

Regulations and Requirements

As described under "Financing the Project," much support exists for historic preservationists in the form of special loans, grants, tax breaks, and even laws such as the Mills Act. These are all designed in recognition of the importance of preserving our architectural heritage and with the idea of facilitating the process.

In contrast to these methods of assistance, there are numerous draconian rules and regulations in place that impede progress in this field and discourage even the best-intentioned historic preservationists. These need to be changed through citizen action that demands adjustments in legislation. One ironic, but positive aspect of today's financial crisis may be that the government entities enforcing unnecessary or exaggerated regulations may find themselves without funding and, as a result, many of these requirements may be abandoned.

In the meantime, however, and for as long as I've been in the business, there have been and still are instances in which it can be easier and cheaper to build something new than to restore an older building. In this way, regulation has contributed to sprawl development, because developers find it is easier and less expensive to build new and out rather than comply with all the restrictions attached to restorations. For example, when building on raw farmland, they don't have to deal with issues like interior toxic clean-up, asbestos abatement, seismic retrofitting, and other restrictions that preservationists are up against.

The cumbersome, costly regulations for restorations did not come about because city planners and architectural preservationists are bad people. They're not. But in my experience, the majority are inexperienced in the nitty-gritty processes involved in building, renovation, and development. Most are well-meaning college graduates who, for the most part, have never had to negotiate a price with an owner, approach a bank for a loan, buy a building and renovation supplies, hire contractors, adhere to building and government requirements, and find tenants. Their educations have been at a desk, not in the field. Additionally, these planners are responding to dated general plans and policies by councils and government. This fact and the politics of development are huge limitations that can result in bad decision making as described in "City Planning."

Some restrictive limitations are due to extreme preservationists who say, "We must restore our historic buildings; I don't care how much it costs; I don't care how many rules we give you; I don't care if the bank doesn't give you a loan, and I don't care that you can't find a tenant because you don't have parking. I want that old building to look just like the old cigar store it used to be."

This kind of thinking is anathema to maintaining our architectural heritage. Usually a restored cigar store is not what a neighborhood needs, but if that store is transformed for use as a business with a current purpose, such as a computer supply center, a café, or a floral shop, then it can maintain a historic look while serving a utilitarian purpose. To restore buildings only for their original purposes is inefficient and illogical. Needs change and buildings can adapt.

Obstacles also proliferate (especially in California) regarding the actual renovations required to bring a building up to code. I'm not against making properties safe, secure, and accessible. But some regulations are clearly excessive, one example of which was the ceiling regulation for the restaurant I described at the end of "The House of the Future."

Another significant example is that because a school was destroyed in an earthquake fifty years ago, old schools with good infrastructures all over the state are being torn down and replaced by new schools retrofitted for earthquakes and prepped for any number of other possible catastrophes. It would be much more efficient to restore the old schools containing infrastructure and constructed with better materials than we use today than building entirely new schools while sacrificing the money that could be applied to education. This new building spree is going on now thanks to the Field Act.

When a building survives the Loma Prieta and all other earthquakes over the past hundred years, and it has no cracks or evidence of settling, one can assume it's a good strong building. However, even for buildings that have weathered the test of time, the state still mandates seismic retrofitting. (And if a government entity is in there, ironically, there are more regulations than for the private sector. They think they need more protection than other businesses). One is forced to spend money to make "improvements" that will not add to a property being more rentable.

Rules regarding the clean-up of things that are not hazardous to health are excessive. For example, encapsulated asbestos that may be ingrained in battleship linoleum takes a jackhammer to get out; it is not a danger to anyone. Another form of asbestos, friable asbestos, is dangerous. A distinction should be made between the two. The same holds true for lead paint. When ingested by children, it is poisonous. However, if one is renovating a building and creating office units in which children will spend little or no time, and the lead paint has been covered by layers of non-lead paint, then it is not a real danger.

Additionally, the major issue for the disabled is to have accessibility to every part of a building. This accessibility need not be compromised, and it could save tremendous cost, if specially designed restrooms were made available not on every floor, but on every other floor where they would be accessible by elevator. Such a simple accommodation could make the difference in whether or not a developer can afford to carry through on a much-needed renovation. Flexibility in approaching the question of accessibility is necessary if our historic architecture is to be preserved and utilized. Otherwise, with overly stringent regulations, everyone loses.

Is it better for anyone, the able-bodied or the disabled, to see the deterioration of a beautiful town because building requirements could not be modified in reasonable ways? It's possible to create solutions that are beneficial to the overall health of a community and are still inclusive.

We should do our best to be as safe as possible from most of the circumstances we are likely to encounter inside or outside a structure. But if we spend all our time dictated by absolutes, we won't be able to save our cities and towns or create decent lifestyles for ourselves and our children.

Regulations are like having an angel on one shoulder and a devil on the other. It's such a delicate balance; you don't want to be completely unregulated because unsafe buildings will be constructed, but you don't want regulations so excessive that good developers are chased away. A balance must be reached between spending to create safe, solid structures and an overabundance of spending to create buildings meant to withstand any and all calamities to which nature and mankind might subject them.

By lightening up a little on excessive regulations, we can make building and rebuilding more affordable while freeing up more money to pay for things we as a society need: better education, health care, and an improvement in our quality of life.

SIX URBAN BUILDING BLOCKS

- ❒ Choosing a Project
- ❒ Financing
- ❒ Design Considerations
- ❒ Finding Tenants
- ❒ Public/Private Partnerships
- ❒ Regulations and Requirements

The Victorians

"What does preservation preserve? You might say it honors peculiarity, specific to the building and to the locality."
Stewart Brand, *How Buildings Learn*

Introduction

Most historical communities in America contain examples of mid-nineteenth and early twentieth century Victorian architecture, with its profusion of bays, cupolas, and dentil work in a cacophony of styles. Originally homes for shop owners, bankers, judges, and merchants, these buildings expressed the uniqueness and creativity of the American spirit. The designs were so popular that for those unable to afford custom-built homes, Victorian architecture could be ordered through catalogs at lower costs. Carpenters and artisans would then provide distinctive embellishments to the basic structures in wood, brick, and stone.

Although the exteriors of Victorian homes were complex, they were structurally quite simple. In California, many were poised on redwood sills on top of dirt or brick foundations. Neighborhoods of Victorians, replete with lush gardens, boulevards, and ample play areas for children, embodied the very best qualities of city living on a human scale. With the housing shortages of the 1940s and the migration to the suburbs, many of these grand Victorians were divided and converted into apartments.

Fortunately, in large cities like San Francisco, the 1960s heralded the beginning of a new approach to restoring older buildings. There was a reclaiming of Victorian and other types of architecture, and then a re-adaptation of these structures to diverse uses. Some were retrofitted with modern light fixtures,

Hunter Street Victorian in the Magnolia Historic District, Stockton.

electrical systems, heating and air-conditioning systems, and reconverted from apartments back into single-family dwellings. Others morphed into multi-use offices, retail, and specialty environments.

These projects marked the beginning of a larger restoration movement, in which Americans experimented with reutilization, recycling, and quality of design. As a teenager, I was intrigued and impressed by the dramatic changes in the San Francisco Fillmore district, where renewed Victorians became the model for entry-level historic development.

Design Considerations

Typically, the more extensive changes took place in building interiors. Small parlors were opened up and became spacious living areas. Kitchens were enlarged to accommodate a more relaxed family life. Old carpet would be ripped out and pine floors polished. The exteriors required more cosmetic changes, such as multiple color schemes and new woodwork, including decks that would accent the readapted interiors.

When I was ready to do my first restoration—that is, one that required a loan—I chose an old Victorian in Stockton. Although I hadn't been around during the city's Victorian heyday and didn't know the specific histories attached to those homes, I based my renovations on what I'd seen in cities such as San Francisco, Portland, and Seattle.

When working with Victorians, be aware that it's difficult to replicate unique accoutrements, like moldings and plinth blocks around windows. Stick machines, which are big cast iron mechanisms that can make copies of a specific trim or pieces of molding, exist but are rare. The solution is to save everything from the original structure, then strip, refinish, and replace it. Redwood, which ostensibly will last forever, should be sanded, then primed and up to five coats of good paint applied. You want the paint job to last, because the investment of time and money can be very high when recreating the decorative facades of what were referred to as painted ladies or Queen Annes. I would usually use up to five colors on a Victorian to enhance its ornamental style.

San Joaquin Street Victorian in the Magnolia Historic District, Stockton.

Financing and Regulations

In addition to loans, there are specific grants and funding sources available for historic preservation. In Stockton, I along with several other stalwart souls, got the neighborhood in which we were renovating Victorians designated a national historic district. This allowed consideration for federal programs that offer special grants and low-interest loans for historic renovations. The designation also qualified it for grants administered through the state parks.

However, these funds come with conditions, so becoming a historic landmark can be useful and an honor for some and a scary thing for others. On the one hand, being honored by committees, commissions, and government authorities is positive and inspires others to renovate and restore old buildings. On the other hand, it can impose limitations, such as being prohibited from converting a building to a new use.

1035 North Monroe Street

As I described in the first chapter, I was in my early twenties when I bought my first Victorian. My second purchase, at 1035 North Monroe, was also a Victorian. One of the older buildings in the San Joaquin Valley, much of it had been transported around Cape Horn circa 1874. Its most recent incarnation had been a kind of retirement home, and it was redolent of many decades of families before that. It was a very special place.

I purchased it with a fellow teacher at the middle school where I taught. We paid equal parts of the cost and the mortgage in what's called a Tenants in Common (TIC) arrangement. This was unusual at the time. It was a big house, so we split it. I lived downstairs and he lived upstairs. It was a good arrangement.

Later I bought many Victorians and converted them primarily into offices, for which there was a high demand in the early 1970s. Many of these homes were available for about $30,000, and even though my rents were low, they still generated enough money to cover my costs.

Remuddling

The neighborhood, however, did not become revitalized in the way I'd hoped. I could not overcome the damage that had been done in the fifties and sixties, when many of the deteriorating Victorians had been torn down and replaced by high-density apartment buildings put up with little city oversight. Setbacks (distances required by law from the edge of a building to the property line) were often very limited and, in many cases, people could reach out and touch the building next door. There weren't adequate play areas for kids, and the natural rhythm of the streets was disrupted. Families moved out, and transients and people with alcohol and drug-related problems moved in. Abandoned cars took the place of rose bushes and aluminum siding replaced wooden exteriors. Those of us dedicated to restoration call this *remuddling*.

Summary

Turning this neighborhood around proved to be very difficult. Had overlay zoning been applied before renovation began, or even better, before deterioration set in, that would have been very helpful. Overlay zoning is a regulatory tool that creates a special zoning district placed over an existing base zone that identifies additional provisions to the base district. For example, if this neighborhood, which was originally zoned only for residential use, had been able to use overlay zoning to include commercial use, then it would allow for more stores, markets, restaurants, and retail activity, and residents could both live and work there.

Working with this particular Stockton neighborhood taught me a lot about why specific projects succeed or fail and the importance of good city planning and management. When I moved on to larger building ventures, this knowledge served me well as I acquired the new skills needed for more complex projects.

Heritage Square

"New usages persistently retire or reshape buildings. From the first drawings to the final demolition, buildings are shaped and reshaped by changing cultural currents, changing real estate value and changing usage."

Stewart Brand, *How Buildings Learn*

Coming Full Circle

In a prior life as a graduate student in education, I taught in a Catholic school, then named San Joaquin Middle School, as part of the required curriculum for my degree. Constructed in the 1930s, the handsome two-story, 25,000 square-foot beaux-arts building housed grammar, middle, and high schools—St. Agnes, S. J. Middle, and St. Mary's, respectively. There was an adjacent building that served as a convent for the teaching nuns of the Franciscan order.

I needed a teaching position before I'd received a credential, and S. J. Middle hired me, an Old Testament guy, to teach social studies and English, coach their sports teams, and play guitar at Mass. What was so terrific about this experience was that, although we came from different backgrounds, teachers and administrators were all united in a common cause—to offer the best education possible to the diverse, inner-city student body, and to create community in the process.

St. Agnes High School, circa 1930s. Courtesy the Bank of Stockton Historical Photograph Collection.

I taught at S. J. Middle for three years and fully enjoyed the experience. However, during my tenure there, I made the decision to forego a teaching career for one in restoration. I had already restored several Victorians, and as I became more acquainted with the problems in Stockton caused by sprawl, I thought my energy would be better applied to full-time architectural restoration in the inner city. I was also considering the future for my family and thought I would have more control providing for them as an entrepreneur and preservationist than I would as a middle school teacher.

Choosing a Project

Six years after leaving S. J. Middle, I noticed the school had gone out of business, and plywood covered the exterior walls. The diocese did not have the funds to keep the school. What does one do with a big empty schoolhouse with a yard, half a dozen basketball courts, no parking lot, and an adjacent convent? Clearly, I wasn't the only one having a problem envisioning a use for this—a real estate broker had been working for three years trying to find an acceptable offer. The situation saddened me, not just for the loss of the school, but also because in a then-city of 170,000 people, no one could think of a suitable use for a school building and a convent.

Finally in 1984, I made an offer on the building for $500,000. Since this was approximately a $300,000 reduction from what they were asking, I thought that was the last I'd hear of it. Well, they accepted the offer. Now I had a building with plywood-covered walls of my very own. It was amazing how creative I got all at once.

Financing – Swing Dance

I didn't have the money—I almost never had the money—but I knew I had to figure out a way to make it work. So, I got a swing loan (also called a mezzanine loan) through the Bank of Stockton that allowed me to buy the buildings.

One way to purchase a building is to get a line of credit. You have money right away, but you also have to secure the loan with your own assets.

An alternative is a swing loan, which gives you kind of a line of credit secured by the property. A swing loan allows you to purchase the building and make improvements while awaiting appraisals. Once the reconstruction is complete and you have a tenant, the bank comes in, and if all is well, offers a loan at 70 or 80 percent of the appraised value. This is the final, or take out loan, and it is usually long-term.

S.J. Middle School, all boarded up. Courtesy the Bank of Stockton Historical Photograph Collection.

Finding Tenants for the Convent

With the finances in order, I now had two buildings that had served quite different functions—the school and the convent. As I've mentioned, the tenant may be the most important piece of the restoration puzzle. In this case, I had the perfect tenant in mind for the old convent building.

I knew that the Stockton Women's Center was considering moving out of the two houses they then occupied into a larger space. The combined square footage of their houses was about half the size of the 9,000 square-foot convent. The convent was a lovely building with stained glass windows and an interior that exuded quiet and serenity. What more perfect way to fill a space that had been inhabited by women living in a spiritual community than with another group whose purpose was to support women in need of help or protection from abuse?

◘ Lot Line Adjustment

Linda, the director of the center, happened to be a friend of mine who had also been employed in the Catholic school system. She agreed that it was a good match, and, after some negotiation, we settled on a mutually beneficial agreement. The center would sell its houses and buy the convent if the convent property was separated from the school property. To accomplish this, I used a lot line adjustment, which basically split the land into two parcels, each with a building on it. A lot line adjustment is not a perfunctory process. It usually begins with a surveyor, and then proceeds through the local community development department, and fire and public works departments. All have to agree that each building meets all the requirements of a separate entity, such as proper setbacks and appropriate fire exits.

After the lot line adjustment on the property was completed, the Women's Center purchased the convent for $250,000. It was a perfect solution for both of us, and an illustration of what can happen through a good partnership. You never know what the potential might be; a prospective tenant may want to purchase a space, immediately or down the road, or there may be another arrangement that would benefit each party. It's important to find appropriate tenants, to think creatively, and to keep an open mind.

Following page: The convent building was transformed into the Women's Center of San Joaquin County.

Design Considerations

After selling the convent, I only had the school property to worry about and a $250,000 debt. I spent approximately $300,000 to readapt the school to an office and commercial-use space while maintaining some of the classrooms, the auditorium, and the cafeteria. Since the building still embodied the character of a school, it required some modifications to be ready for a new use.

❐ Creating an Architectural Identity

Restorers should aim to create an architectural identity, which brands a property as something unique and intriguing. To readapt this 1930s vintage building, we made several cosmetic but effective changes, completely altering the look of the old school.

The first task was to dispense with the old school's institutional character, evident in the harsh fluorescent lighting, green walls, and dull carpeting. We stripped, sanded, and finished the Oregon hard pine floors, then put down a colorful carpet in the center of the hallways to muffle sound and reduce wear and tear. We replaced the fluorescent lights with a more energy-efficient system bordered by mahogany trim which gave an art deco, mid-century flavor to the structure. We pulled out the bookcases, stripped off layers of old paint, refinished them to make the mahogany look new, and put them back in place.

Similarly, columns were stripped. An artist painted them to look like marble, contributing to the ambiance we sought. We added up-to-date heating, air conditioning, electrical and plumbing systems and fulfilled the requirements of the Americans with Disabilities Act. The old playground was converted into a one hundred-car parking lot. When we were finished, it was an elegant, utilitarian restoration with an art deco look.

To draw tenants to an inner-city space, this level of attention to the presentation, feel, and utility of a building is essential. Other practical considerations, such as adequate parking and good outdoor lighting, are also necessary. Tenants must feel they are coming into a beautiful, safe environment that their clients or customers would also feel comfortable entering.

Finding Tenants for the Renovated School Building

When the building was ready, I cast as wide a net as possible in the pursuit of tenants. My first and anchor tenant was the Private Industry Council, an organization that helped people find jobs. They had contacted me about renting the first floor as an educational center. To their specifications, I converted the classrooms into combination small offices and teaching environments, while they invested a significant amount of money to install two hundred new telephone lines. (This was before fiber optics.)

❒ A Love Story

With my mortgage payments met, it was now time to make some cash on this deal. This required finding a use for the second floor. I had to get creative, because there was no elevator, which brings me to a little diversion.

One day a local broker called me with the possibility of a new tenant for the second floor. A ballet school was interested in renting the old science classrooms. I happened to be late for the appointment with the broker and the prospective tenant, so I ran up the stairs, did a pirouette to lighten the moment and nearly landed on my chin. I'm not sure I impressed Elizabeth, the lovely young owner/director of the ballet school, but she impressed me. I sat down with her and the real estate agent and they described their needs.

They wanted it to look like the Bolshoi Ballet building in 1938 Moscow. The only proximity to that would be the age of the building; nothing else fit the bill.

Enchanted by Elizabeth and desperate for a tenant, I agreed to take a look at a postcard she had brought illustrating the design she wanted. Hoping this renovation would be a catalyst to entice more tenants, I moved full speed ahead into refinishing the old hard pine floors on the second floor, sheet rocking, faux painting the new rose-colored walls, installing mirrors, iron brackets and wood bars, redoing the cast iron radiators, and installing a window air conditioning system. Finally, to much public fanfare, we opened up our own Bolshoi Ballet, Stockton style. The Stockton Ballet School became my tenant, and Elizabeth became my wife.

Cars would pull into the parking lot, in what was previously a very rough neighborhood, to drop off young, upper-middle class girls in tutus. We were able to move county office users into the rest of the second floor, and the building was once again full and bustling with activity. Although we made considerably more improvements for the ballet school than usual, the other tenant improvements for the classrooms were considerably less, and we balanced out at about $25 per square foot. Comparable office space for that type of tenant improvement was approximately $40 per square foot.

Regulations

This project was eased by a state policy called the California Historic Building Code, which applies to buildings over fifty years old. Certain requirements that may be too onerous for a building of that age are waived, such as having to add an extra fire escape or a new electrical system.

Summary

Four or five years ago, the Stockton Unified School District bought Heritage Square, and it has become a school again. It had morphed from a Catholic school when it was built in the early twentieth century to a public school at the beginning of the twenty-first century.

When I acquired the building in 1984, I approached school board after school board suggesting they buy the building and use it for what it was meant to be. I brought the Stockton Unified School District in numerous times, saying, "You're building a six million dollar new school, and for a couple of million, I can sell you a renovated school. I could make this better than anything you could do." But my logical, cost-effective suggestions fell on deaf ears. I had to manifest the vision first. Only years later did it dawn on them that it was a good idea.

Heritage Square, as a mixed-use building, maintained the flavor of a school with the utility of an office for many years. The cafeteria and auditorium were incorporated into its use. Because of this utility, Heritage Square remained fully and continuously occupied after its restoration. I consider this a very successful project that belatedly has rediscovered its proper identity. It became an excellent example of show and tell.

Eden Square

"Convivial towns can offer solace in disaster, solidarity in protest, and a quiet everyday delight in urban life....Creating and revitalizing places that foster conviviality is essential to the good life."
Mark C. Childs

The Urban Village

Eden Square was one of our most important projects. It paved the way for similar environments, such as Cort Tower and Railroad Square, and was a prime opportunity to utilize my show-and-tell tactics for the city of Stockton, which was unaware of the emerging urban village concept.

The urban village idea embodied a new approach to the development of commercial and residential spaces. Conceived both as an alternative to sprawl and to what some considered the impersonal qualities of city life, it began to take shape during the mid-eighties. About that time, a think tank was formed at Stanford that included some of the most qualified, forward-thinking professionals in the fields of architecture, city planning, business, and finance to consider the future of American cities. Their conclusion was that the best approach to saving our cities was by creating multi-use downtown and midtown buildings, preferably by restoring and readapting existing structures.

In addition to readapting buildings and specific areas, the idea was to provide environments in which there would be less reliance on cars (therefore a decrease in oil consumption and a smaller carbon footprint) and more on public transit, bicycles and walking. Communities would be compact and self-sustaining; public places to gather and socialize would be key elements. Residents would feel safer, spend less time in their cars and more with family and friends, and enjoy better physical and emotional health while conserving natural resources.

Eden Square

Cort Tower

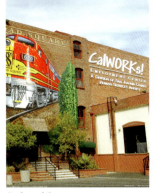
Railroad Square

To my contra-developer's mind, this was a terrific antidote to sprawl and embodied all the salient elements related to preserving historic architecture and recreating community in cities. Urban villages, as I viewed them, were very similar to the model of the intact neighborhoods of San Francisco, such as Chinatown, Richmond, and North Beach, each self-sufficient with a character all its own.

The style also allowed for adaptation into a number of village forms. This and the following chapters describe our creation of three distinct types of urban villages.

Eden Square, our first and most comprehensive, became a mixed-use facility that included residential and commercial space. Cort Tower was designed to be a downtown urban office village that included businesses and services of all kinds, a health club, and restaurant. Finally, Railroad Square is a community outreach urban village for public services.

New Urbanism

There are a couple of philosophies about how to approach urban life for the future. New urbanists are those who say, "I'm going to build a whole new city and it's going to look a lot like ancient Greece. It's going to have everything you need in terms of living and work spaces, retail, entertainment, parks, etc." Many of these communities have been and continue to be established. It's a popular concept.

New urbanism endorses replication of what exists as our historic architecture. It copies a city's gabled and lofted architecture, adding to it all the modern amenities. Unfortunately, new urbanism requires new construction. Though significantly more efficient than outskirts development, it doesn't utilize what is already built or historic building materials, nor is it accented by the unique craftsmanship of our forebears. While it presents a historic appearance, an essential contact with the past—touching an actual historic structure that reverberates with so many stories—is not satisfied.

Although these developers are well-intentioned and include parks, pubs, and open public spaces in their designs, there are cities with existing infrastructures prime for revitalization that are languishing. In contrast to new urbanists, a contra-developer's process is similar to that of an archeologist in that we both deal with the ruins of cities. No one would think of abandoning the ruins of a historic city in Europe, but here we abandon, destroy, and demolish our old architecture to create brand new "historic" environments.

The urban villages I endorse don't copy what used to be a really good city. Rather, they are the result of reinvigorating and reinventing an existing city by salvaging the existing architecture and infrastructure, and then enticing a new and vigorous community of tenants.

A Brief History of Eden Square

In the 1930s, California State Senator Frank Boggs built an apartment building of approximately 70,000 square feet that he called Eden Square. It was a monolithic structure designed in a Romanesque, neoclassical style with terra cotta and marble adornments and colonnades. In form, it was a precursor to the urban village. The first floor housed a floral shop, an AAA office, and a café. There was also an underground garage. On the upper floors, Boggs built apartments and invited his friends to rent from him, a practice that was customary at that time for people of his social status.

On the sixth floor, he built a penthouse for himself overlooking the San Joaquin River Deep Water Channel, replete with gardens and a small orchard of oranges, lemons, and other trees. (Boggs was instrumental in having the channel dredged, making it safe for large cargo ships to come into Stockton's inland harbor.) During its heyday, Eden Square's large studios and one-bedroom apartments were home to many of the city's most famous retirees, widowers, and gadflies, whom Boggs enjoyed entertaining in his sixth-floor bachelor pad.

A fire gutted the building in the late thirties. It was restored, but only to the fifth floor. I wasn't even aware of Boggs' sixth-floor penthouse until after I researched the building's history in the Stockton public library.

But Eden Square never truly rebounded from the fire. There was a succession of owners following Senator Boggs' death, and it performed adequately for several years, but never as well as in its salad days. As more of Stockton's aged elite moved to waterfront communities and assisted living apartments, properties like this fell into disrepair.

By 1989, its owners of five years were perplexed about what to do with it. They had tried to lease out the apartments but had done little clean up, and there were vacant commercial units on the first floor. Not surprisingly, they were unable to keep it occupied except by a few individuals of very limited means. And there was no city plan for neighborhood development on which to rely for guidance.

Courtesy the Bank of Stockton Historical Photograph Collection.

Choosing the Project

When I learned that year that the property was for sale, I made a tour of the premises, and it was clear why it had been on the market for so long. The whole interior was run down. Of the thirty-six apartment units, ten were occupied, all by young, unemployed (read: unemployable) incorrigibles high on something or about to be. Approximately a city-block long, it was constructed of concrete with reinforced brick and was five stories high scaling down to one-and-a-half on the south commercial end. I discovered thousands of square feet of unused space and little rooms with opaque doors—home, I heard, to some of Stockton's notorious gumshoes.

On my second visit, the place was surrounded by police cars. Perhaps on a dare, an inebriated young man walking blindfolded across an air vent on the roof covered only with a thick layer of wire mesh, had fallen five stories to the ground. In keeping with Leo Durocher's famous observation that God watches over drunks and third basemen, the guy actually survived, breaking his legs and one elbow.

Not too long after that incident, my mother visited from San Francisco. One evening as we walked by the project, one of its occupants tossed a beer bottle from the fourth floor that shattered in front of her. As several of his buddies on the fire escape doubled up in laughter, my mother screeched, "Please, son, don't buy this place!" (When I finally did purchase the property, the first order of business was serving eviction notices to the few remaining tenants.)

Despite my mother's plea, the property's location at the edge of a rough neighborhood, and its bedraggled condition, Eden Square called to me. I could imagine it converted into a vibrant multi-use structure with an eclectic mix of small businesses on the first floor owned by entrepreneurs who could benefit from lower rents. I envisioned those business owners and others living in the apartment units on the floors above, and residents enrolled in classes on the premises, or having a cup of coffee in a café on the first floor. I could see tenants taking their kids for a walk in the park across the street. A comprehensive facility with easy access to a multitude of services in a place where people felt at home—that was exactly the model I wanted to create and see duplicated throughout the country. If I could make this work, then others would follow. Of course, the concept of an affordable urban village wasn't on most people's radar at the time, especially in Stockton. The challenges would be huge, but what an opportunity!

❐ A Magical Moment

I was still mulling over whether to take on those many challenges when one day, on a visit to the building, I tried to open an interior door that had been shut for many years. It was stuck, so I gave it a good heave ho and, as it creaked open, a newspaper fell from the door jam into the crook of my arm. Its front page read: "MacArthur Returns," and the date was April 11, 1951—the date of my birth. I decided then to buy the property.

Each building speaks to you in its own way. If you've done your homework on the property, and you encounter a magic moment like this one, let it guide you. They have always pointed me in the right direction.

Financing

The price was $1.1 million, and the financing got a little complicated. I had to get a loan to buy the building, but most lenders prefer to facilitate either commercial or residential developers, not both. I went to the Bank of Stockton and they agreed to a loan of $700,000 based on its residential use. This wasn't enough for the project, so I secured a second mortgage of $400,000 from another bank based on the property's commercial value.

I also needed money to make tenant improvements and, with the help of an investor and some of my own money, I was able to cover those.

The building was 100 percent financed (usually banks like to finance about 70 percent of the appraised value or sales price, whichever is less), but my own money went into the improvements. In the nomenclature of development, this is called a workout. A workout is designed to assuage the concerns of banks that the buyer might drop the ball in the middle of the project and walk away. The workout in this case was the use of non-institutional, non-bank funding plus sweat equity to complete the improvements to the building. The new value would be approximately $2 million, and with 70 percent of that, I would be able to pay off the first loan.

The private investor was a longtime family friend who was retiring from his jewelry business in Sacramento and looking to invest in something that would bring him a good return. He became a partner. The agreement was that he would loan me money to do tenant improvements and I'd pay him interest and get the principle back to him first. Then, when I sold it, he'd get a percentage. As it turned out, we didn't sell it during the partnership. I bought him out with a good profit, and he was very happy.

He got a good write-off, depreciation, and appreciation in addition to the many other benefits that come with buying a historic building.

His contribution was pivotal. He was an older man investing money into a building he remembered from his childhood. This made his participation more significant than if he'd been just another investor. As he created relationships with tenants by calling, visiting or just loving them up a little, his post-retirement years became imbued with meaning and satisfaction. And his kind attention helped tenants to have a sense of belonging in the newly forming village.

❐ Condominiumization

We wanted to offer apartment residents the opportunity to own their units, so we created a plan to make that available. Based on the financing and the sale price, we would be able to sell the residential units as condominiums for approximately half the price of the newer condos in town. Stockton, considered a city in need, qualified for Community Reinvestment Act (CRA) funds that were geared toward creating inexpensive housing for first-time homebuyers, young people, seniors, and minorities. There were also lots of very fair residential, below-market loan deals to be had, making it affordable for people with moderate incomes to buy a home. The bank agreed to finance through their Small Business Association programs. We also condominiumized the commercial spaces. Thus, with a few transactions, an enterprising businessperson could efficiently buy a commercial condominium, finance a business, and purchase a home unit on the upper floors.

The consequences were groundbreaking. Women, minorities, and the underserved of the community would have the advantages of home and business ownership. Remarkably, the city was very easy to deal with regarding the transition from a single-owner-occupied, multi-use building, to a multi-owned, multi-use building.

Finding Tenants

Even though it wasn't the best neighborhood, Eden Square was close enough to the University of the Pacific and the Miracle Mile shopping center that there was a good chance we could make it enticing to tenants who wanted something a little different or edgy. Bringing in good tenants would improve the entire area. I had some ideas about people in town who might be interested and I courted them by offering reduced rents and letting them know that I would build to suit. I employed the show-and-tell technique of architectural renderings

to help prospective tenants visualize renovated units. That, and the promise of below-market rents, worked well in attracting good occupants.

The first and anchor tenant was an aikido school that had been located in town. The owners also rented two living facilities, and eventually some of their teachers and students moved into apartments as well. We worked on both the commercial and residential properties at the same time. When it was completed, the aikido school, with its large street frontage, provided an ambiance of security and utility that was reassuring to other tenants.

Next, I pursued a café owner who installed a very nice European café on the first floor, and he and his employees also rented several apartments. The combination of the school and the café, with its tasty offerings, helped me close the next large anchor tenant: a child daycare center. One of my reasons for wanting such a center was that nurses working at Dameron Hospital six blocks away would sometimes leave their children in their cars while they worked because there was nowhere else to place them. We built a 24-hour daycare facility for infants to eight-year-olds. Other early tenants included a senior daycare facility (built adjacent to the children's center) and a garden shop.

Design Considerations

As I've mentioned, this was a perfect show-and-tell opportunity for me to educate Stockton about what an urban village looked like and how it could function. It was necessary to make Eden Square attractive and inviting right away. Although exterior changes were not extensive, they were effective in altering the property's image. We installed black awnings with gold lettering, cleaned the terra cotta, washed down the brick, and painted the woodwork; these moderate changes endowed the building with a respectable and dignified visage. Then we went to work on the inside, where construction demands were substantial.

I went to school on this project. (It was akin to a bachelor's program in large building renovation while Cort Tower, which I completed later, was more like my master's program.) There were many factors to consider for a property of this size that I had not previously encountered, including choosing and maintaining elevators both for passengers and freight, installing air conditioning and sprinkler systems, and meeting all the health and safety codes. These were major hurdles and great learning opportunities.

We met all the requirements and constructed spaces for individual tenants, assisting them with several improvements, including lofts and bathrooms. We also redesigned access ways and opened up the building to create a comfortable flow between the commercial and residential areas.

❐ From Auto Shop to Daycare Center: An Ingenious Design

One of the biggest transformations was the daycare center, for which we generated an innovative design.

There had been an auto shop/garage on the first floor. It was essentially a big old warehouse that had suffered from years of neglect. The first task was to remove all the lifts and other machinery. We gutted and cleaned out the space, leaving the outer brick walls up. Then we built another enclosed environment inside with four walls of its own and a ceiling. Between the interior and exterior walls, we installed the steel bracing that satisfied seismic regulations and the other required systems to meet the vast body of codes for a child daycare center. This left the entire 10,000 square feet of the center pristine for play and nap areas, kept the retrofitting and other systems invisible, and maintained the historic flavor of the building by preserving its brick façade.

Our next tenant was a senior daycare facility that was constructed adjacent to the children's daycare center. This juxtaposition led to some wonderful interactions in which the able seniors befriended the kids, playing with them and taking them on little walks inside the premises. There were even a couple of instances in which a tenant family concurrently had a parent using the senior center and a child enrolled in the daycare center. To my mind, this epitomizes the support, security, and nurturing that an urban village is able to provide.

Summary

The most important qualities of Eden Square superseded its location and its exterior beauty. Its essence derived from the combination of people who lived and worked there and the ways in which they interacted. When you have seniors playing with children, business owners living and working in a building, friends meeting at the café for a cup of coffee, and students taking classes at the aikido studio, there's enough happening right there to engender a sense of home and responsibility—and to identify a place as a village.

When people feel at home and supported within a community, what follows in the natural course of events are fundamental changes in the roles they play. Many of those benefiting from this village lifestyle can and do become citizen-lobbyists in their cities. They begin to demand quality city planning. They take action to stop crime and keep public areas clean and safe. They fight against big-box stores on the outskirts of town because now there's a sense of ownership for a community, which translates into a desire to keep it healthy. All these factors compel city officials to respond with good planning.

In Eden Square, I was willing to take the time and trouble to craft something that was more valuable as the sum of its parts—thirty-six condominiums and 30,000 square feet of commercial space—than as a single building. My goal was to create an urban village that would be a model and an inspiration to others to produce their own similarly comprehensive environments. This is one of the most important projects we have ever done, and it provided me with a foundation of knowledge in moving forward.

Railroad Square

"Daring ideas are like chessmen moving forward. They may be beaten, but they may start a winning game."
Johan Wolfgang von Goethe

A Social Services Urban Village

It wasn't like I was seeking a project. We were completing Eden Square, and I was looking forward to telling its story on the lecture circuit before taking on anything new. Then I got a call from a local real estate agent soliciting my interest in a "troubled property." Troubled was an understatement.

A Brief History of Railroad Square

This property had an unusual pedigree. It was constructed in 1910 and originally used by the Sunset Door and Sash Company. Remodeled in 1916 for Sears, Roebuck and Co., it became the company's only mail order distribution center in California until 1927. All the inventory, including major machinery, baby carriages, and windmills, that could be purchased from the catalog in the years between 1916 and 1970 had been housed in that warehouse. When I came to Stockton, it was still a showroom for Sears garden supplies and farm equipment.

Railroad Square

At three stories equalling 120,000 square feet, it was one of the largest brick warehouses west of the Mississippi. There was also an additional one-story accessory structure. Built near the railroad tracks for easier offloading of large equipment, it consisted of huge rough-sawn timbers and equally rough brick interiors.

Several years after Sears sold it, there had been a brief flirtation with an insurance organization. They had initiated work on the interior, but it had come to an abrupt halt when some of the construction money mysteriously disappeared, along with the operators.

Worse, the property was the extreme example of the opposite of the well-known dictum of real estate value: "location, location, location." If there's such a thing as an A+ location, it was an F- location. This once noble lady sat amidst weeds and hypodermic needles next to the Southern Pacific railroad tracks in the old industrial section of town. Since the seventies the site had been used as target practice for local thugs and drug enthusiasts, and it had stood vacant for the better part of ten years. With virtually no attraction, no utility, and no location, this building was of questionable sales quality. Naturally, the owners turned to me, the only local contra-developer.

Choosing the Property

Ironically, the owner's possession of the property stemmed from an unfortunate series of incidents. He owned a heating and air conditioning/sheet metal business and had been hired as a contractor by the short-lived insurance company. When the company's funds dried up, this unlucky soul had already spent approximately $300,000 in time and materials on the heating and air conditioning installations and hadn't been paid a dime. In addition, the holder of the first mortgage of roughly $750,000 decided to foreclose.

Faced with losing his investment through the foreclosure,

Photos above and facing page: Courtesy the Bank of Stockton Historical Photograph Collection.

the contractor elected to pay off the first mortgage, which meant the owner had spent over a cool million on this white elephant. Next, he embarked on a fruitless ten-year career marketing this project. From agencies of the United Way to industrial users, the right match remained elusive. Meanwhile, at his ranch home in Livermore over an hour away, his peaceful existence would be frequently shattered by calls from glass vendors, police, and firefighters with reports of bullets splintering windows, arson-set fires, and other assaults to which empty buildings like his are subjected.

On a muggy fall day in 1995, his broker paid me a visit, indicating that his client had suffered enough, and would I pay him $750,000 for the property? Hands gesticulating wildly, he stated that would be a 30 percent reduction on an already low market price. I was so enticed that I ushered him out the door.

Months passed and, crestfallen, he showed up at my office again beseeching me to "get creative." I told him that the only way I'd add this albatross to my portfolio was if the owner gave it to me. Much to my astonishment, he took this "offer" back to his seller. The seller accepted my challenge, agreeing to give me the property in exchange for keeping a percentage interest in it. After several weeks of contemplation, my company decided to take the risk.

Financing, Step One: A Back-end Investment

The broker's plea to get creative was answered in the unique financing arrangements we worked out. As the project progressed, so did the creative financing plans.

Our proposal was one I'd never heard of before (although someone somewhere could have taken a similar tack). I told the owner that he would have to come in on the back end, not the front. Normally I would pay $750,000 up front; it would go through escrow, the owner would convey the property to me, and the transaction would be complete. With our deal, he would give me the property and I'd give him the opportunity to make more money down the road. I offered his broker 6 percent and him 27 percent interest. But, he wouldn't get it until the place was fixed up and rented or sold.

We made up a contract and formed a limited partnership. Immediately after we signed the contract, I took my free and clear property and marched down to the bank for some improvement loans, and was immediately turned down. As was discussed earlier in the book, community reinvestment is not really at the top of the list for most banking institutions. Their preference was a suburban housing development or big box store. As one bank after another refused my request, I sought advice from my home office team. The consensus was that to make the situation viable, we had to land the right tenant.

Finding Tenants

From the beginning I knew we would have to find county tenants because government groups are always looking for big spaces with lots of open floor plans and parking (this property had an acre of parking). Several social service agencies could fit into this structure. Because of its location, it wasn't appropriate for high-end office, retail, or housing, but it could work well for the county.

As a short-term arrangement, however, early on we rented space to the Chamber of Commerce, which used it for incubating new businesses. I rented to them at a very low rate and they had lots of parking. They were a good fit for that time period. Getting tenants into a building fast is very important, and the Chamber was a perfect interim resident.

At about the same time, the Office of Human Resources for the County of San Joaquin recognized the potential of this large, stand-alone property situated at a distance from other buildings to house social

"The opposite of adaptation in buildings is graceless turnover. The usual pattern is for a rapid succession of tenants...leaving nothing that successors can use. Finally no tenant replaces the last one, vandals do their quick work, and broken windows beg for demolition. ... Or the building may be blessed with durable construction and resilient design which can forgive insult and hard swerves of usage. A brick factory from the 1910s, with its intelligent daylighting and abundant space, can stand empty for a decade and still gain value."

Stewart Brand, *How Buildings Learn*

service agencies that were generally not accepted in many neighborhoods. This led to our first county tenant: the Office of Substance Abuse, which included the Pregnant Women's Methadone Treatment Center and other services.

It became our marquee tenant, perfectly suited to Railroad Square. They needed a large space, had difficulty finding an appropriate location, and were supported by a reliable source of state and local revenues. It was another win/win for the city; as the addicts benefited from the services, the city benefited from safer streets and less crime.

These two original tenants were a good start, but we still needed to fine-tune the tenant mix.

The county ultimately took care of that by linking up various agencies that would function well together in close proximity. These included a county alternative school, a drunken driving program, an acupuncture program for drug treatment, a local church, the Alliance of Infants and Mothers (AIM)—a program to teach mothers how to care for their children—and an electrical contractor who traded services for rent.

Even with these agencies in place, only about a third of the total square footage was utilized. That left us with two floors to fill. Now that we had several occupants in place, I managed to get a new loan for the property.

In 1996, we began exchanging letters of intent with CalWorks, a welfare-to-work program newly empowered by the state legislature. We offered them 60,000 square feet. We anticipated that they would have the money to make the improvements, but county programs don't always work that way, so back to the bank we went.

Financing, Step Two: Three-Year, Short-fuse Loan

Although we had the county's promise to rent the entire building, we were turned down once again from several banks when we applied for another $1 million loan to continue construction. We were finally able to borrow the sum for three years from a large regional bank. This effectively made our payments around $37,000 a month. (We had already borrowed $2 million to work on the first 50,000 to 60,000 square feet at a reasonable interest rate and twenty-year term.)

In order to meet the requirements for the short-fuse improvement loan, we decided upon another unusual agreement, this one regarding rental payment. It was based on the cost of the custom-built tenant improvements for the specific needs of each county agency and the amount we needed to repay the $1 million within the allotted time frame.

To meet the expenses for those initial years, we charged the slightly above-market rate of $1.18 per square foot for the 120,000 square feet property (market rate was about $1). To offset the higher rental rate of the first three years, I offered the county a long-term advantage of a reduction in rent to $0.35 per square foot for the subsequent five years.

Such a low rate was unheard of, and sealed the deal with the county, which was delighted to apply the hundreds of thousands of dollars in savings on rent to social service programs. CalWorks occupied the entire second and third floors and has been a tenant ever since. The plan worked out perfectly for me too. I was able to meet my payments and make a profit.

Design Considerations

First, to stop the locals from using the building for target practice, we hired an ornamental ironwork company to construct an elegant wrought iron fence around the whole block. It was expensive, but it immediately improved the appearance and also kept the vandals out.

The city of Stockton offers a program called façade loans. These are forgivable loans of up to $15,000 to improve the exterior of properties in the city's blighted districts. With a façade loan we replaced every bullet-riddled window, painted the trim, and added hunter green canvas awnings over the doorways. We renamed the project Railroad Square and started marketing the charm of being a whistle stop. This renaming was a key identifier for the property, keeping it from simply being perceived as just a big restored, brick building. The name Railroad Square

distinguished the whole enterprise, and the artwork it inspired produced the strongest possible presence.

The entire 60,000 square foot restoration took only five months. This was a Herculean task, considering that we started with a rough shell with non-level particle board floors and brick walls with big beam supports. It was just a big, old, empty storage place. We met county guidelines (much more extensive than for the private sector) for seismic retrofitting, handicap accessibility, heat and air conditioning systems, state-of the art wiring, classroom and lighting regulations, and every conceivable health and safety requirement. At the same time, we sandblasted brick, produced multi-color paint jobs and tiled floors, installed computer networks and Internet service, all the while accentuating the elements that emphasized what the building used to be, including visible painted ducting to maintain an industrial look, exposed historic brick, wide doorways, and a functioning old freight elevator.

Everything was new and up to code. This did result in some design compromises, such as a lowered ceiling in one case and sheetrock covering some brick walls. But all in all, the end result was a spectacular combination of landmark architecture, modern amenities, and an ideal mixed-use tenant group. Railroad Square became a social services urban village.

❐ Railroad Square: The Perfect Identifier

As I've mentioned, I have a long-term commitment to include art in my buildings and to offer it in public places. The Railroad Square mural is one of my favorite images created for my properties. It captures the precise qualities I had in mind when the idea began to form in my imagination.

Prior to my completion of the facility for CalWorks, I contacted world-renowned local muralist Carlos Lopez. It was important that people driving by would easily identify the property as Railroad Square. What better way to do that than with the image of a train crashing through the bricks? In this way, I also wanted to symbolize a new day in this East Stockton location with the premises fully occupied and the county agencies up and running. But we had to find the right train.

Carlos and I spent months looking for just the right image, poring over hundreds of pictures in libraries and museums in search of the perfect train. We finally hit upon a gigantic, silver and red, art-deco design. Even though it represented a train designed and utilized mid-century and

Railroad Square was constructed in 1910, we took artistic license and appropriated it as the model for the mural.

Supporting artists (many of them local) by featuring their work in and on my buildings is one of the things that makes my job so rewarding. When I begin a project, I know I'll be making decisions all along the way that will add quality and utility to a structure. When it's financed, restored, and the tenants are in place, one's mind can turn to other things. In this case, I took my profit and spent it to have this beautiful image put on a public space. People couldn't believe that in their once-neglected neighborhood, someone would spend that kind of money for them to see something enjoyable when they drove by. It became so emblematic of the neighborhood that the area became the Railroad Square Historic District. This came after more and more people moved there, a new public school was built across the street, and other new life emerged.

Summary

Within two years, the patience of the previous owner and his broker were rewarded. He got a check for nearly $1 million and his brokers received over $60,000 in compensation/commission. In the meantime, while I was renovating the building and had tenants paying rent, he was getting dividends on his share in the form of monthly interest payments. In the end, everyone was happy with the arrangement.

Going into this ravaged neighborhood and creating a vital village like Railroad Square is all and more than one can ever expect from this profession, and it's good business. Good business means making a community better than you found it, and by doing that, your rewards will come. It's your public service; it takes the restoration development beyond bricks and mortar.

Railroad Square has been immensely successful as a social services center. Its presence contributes in numerous ways to the county, city, and neighborhood by giving people with serious problems a chance to rehabilitate themselves and become active, positive members of the community. The key for Railroad Square was establishing the right tenant mix.

Every community has these old industrial behemoths languishing on the wrong side of the tracks. The challenge is to bring economy and occupancy to these properties so they are able to function as anchors for the neighborhood. If large industrial buildings remain vacant, they attract criminals, graffiti artists, and drug users. Once they are fixed up and full of life, they can provide an economic jump-start for the neighborhood.

Meeting room combines modern and historic elements.

Cort Tower

"We will neglect our cities to our peril, for in neglecting them we neglect the nation."

President John F. Kennedy

It took a year to close the deal on Cort Tower, but it was worth it. This magnificent, ten-story national historic landmark with views of the San Joaquin River was my initiation into central downtown Stockton renovation. From negotiating the price with a large corporation to filling the formidable structure with tenants and creating new interior spaces, this experience paved the way for all my future ventures in downtown development.

It was a structure no one else wanted. But where others perceived a vacuum, I envisioned an opportunity: to revitalize not just one building, but the entire downtown area, devastated by thirty years of development north of the town center.

Stockton's Central Downtown Corridor

Up until the purchase of Cort Tower in 1991, my projects were accomplished in the northern and eastern sections of central Stockton. In the northern section, my work began in the area known as the Magnolia District. This is where all my renovated Victorians, plus Heritage and Eden squares, are located. A group of individuals, myself among them, started Restore Our Inner-city Space and Environment (RISE). We succeeded in getting the entire area rezoned into a national historic district in 1979.

The designation of a national historic district allowed anyone who owned a home or building to avail themselves of special financing and protection, because historic buildings could not be torn down within the district. This has been a great asset to both the city and its residents.

Immediately after completing Eden Square in the north central area, I began to work on Railroad Square in the east area of downtown. Shortly after that, I was drawn to the central downtown corridor by a situation strongly resembling the one we're in today.

After a time of seeming prosperity in the early eighties, the bubble burst and major institutions collapsed, including banks and savings and loans that had written bad loans for years. One of those was American Savings and Loan. By 1990, American's stock had plummeted from $100 a share to $1 a share. At the time, it owned the building that would be renamed Cort Tower.

When I became aware that the Federal Deposit Insurance Corporation (FDIC) had stepped in and forced American to sell its ten-story headquarters, my contra-developer instincts kicked in. I went to look at the structure, and it occurred to me that this downtown corridor, encompassing many buildings with intact infrastructures, had vast potential for revitalization.

I decided to focus my energies here, with the goal of economic and community revitalization. It was an opportunity to educate the city about the potential of these neglected resources. I knew achieving those goals would demand a long-term commitment, because I'd have to do a lot of show-and-tell before the city would comprehend the advantages.

Recent Stockton History

In its prime, Stockton's downtown, like many others in the country, was a vibrant center filled with young people and families, many of whom lived and worked there. They shopped at the local businesses, visited nearby doctors and dentists, and stepped out at night at local clubs and movie theaters. Places had meaning, and people knew each other's stories. The neighbor down the street met her husband at the soda fountain in the Kress Building, cousin Tony opened a shoe repair business on Main Street, and friends walked together to work. Lively interaction, good-natured fun, and assistance in time of need—these were the threads in the fabric of a thriving community.

Facing page: Early downtown Stockton (note the daring wire walker). Courtesy the Bank of Stockton Historical Photograph Collection. Left: new buildings blend with the old in Stockton.

Unfortunately, that sense of community was sacrificed when the city allowed Stockton to sprawl, turning a deaf ear to those who anticipated the environmental, traffic, and crime problems that would ensue. Developers moved north of downtown, bringing the city businesses with them. Exoduses from our city centers, such as this

one, along with irresponsible lending practices, have progressively delivered us into today's mortgage and housing debacle, with close to three out of four homes in foreclosure. Stockton has been used as an example of one of the hardest hit cities in the country as a result of its excessive sprawl development. Where better for a contra-developer to be?

In the late 1970s, while the officers of Grupe Company (a father-son development company and owners of Cort Tower at the time) were choosing new fireplaces for their lavish tenth-floor offices, they were simultaneously creating Lincoln Village West, a housing development that became a first-generation suburb of Stockton. Building led to more building. Farmland was paved over. Walmart, Target and other stores sprung up along the Pacific Avenue corridor. This type of development continued to spread further north, but nobody was thinking about how new roads would be financed, or where the money would come from to pay police officers and firefighters for the new suburbs.

Finally, this seemingly unending expansion prompted warnings from the state attorney general to stop the sprawl or be subject to fines and law suits. The state's officials now understand that sprawl contributes to the depletion of the ozone and pollution of our earth, water and air. The irony is that while city leaders, planners, banks, and others were enjoying the benefits of being in a vital downtown area, their general plan and growth actions encouraging sprawl were precipitating its demise.

This was not immediately apparent in the early 1980s. There was a general feeling of prosperity in the air. But starting in 1987 with the savings and loan crisis, everything came tumbling down due to accelerating interest rates and terrible business practices. The rise in rates and the recession that followed triggered a huge drop in American's stock. Investors lost a lot of money. The failure of our savings and loans institutions isn't new; history repeats itself.

Courtesy the Bank of Stockton Historical Photograph Collection.

"Stockton Someplace Special"

The damage, brewing for so long beneath the surface, had become clearly visible. Stockton's motto, "Stockton Someplace Special," sounded like a joke in 1990. There were a few businesses left downtown, but most had moved out, retail stores had disappeared, there was no theater or entertainment of any kind, and there was a perception of crime. To quote Gertrude Stein, "There was no there there."

However, there were indications that Stockton was ready for a renaissance. City officials were interested in bringing new life to the downtown area at last. (The city would ultimately revitalize the Bob Hope Theatre and build a new events center and baseball field.)

This was the perfect opportunity to initiate a revitalization of the community. Many residents who had moved away from the city center still retained happy memories of better days. Rekindled, their shared histories, invisibly engraved on the city streets and in the city structures, could bring life back to the community and pave the way for new memories.

I perceived several practical draws to encourage the return of businesses that had left and to attract new ones to open. One advantage was that the tower was located in an enterprise zone, and anyone who hires people in an enterprise zone gets tax credits. Also, although downtown had its share of homeless people, vagrants and parolees, it was turf-neutral, meaning there were no gangs. Although there was a perception of crime, the fact was, since gang members stayed away there was less crime downtown than in other parts of the city.

Another unrecognized but important asset was the Crosstown Freeway, located two blocks from the tower. The freeway, built at a cost of $100 million, is one of the few spots in California that connects Interstate 5 and Highway 99, parallel freeways that run the length of the Central Valley and beyond. From it, the looming one hundred forty-five foot Cort Tower is an imposing presence.

A Brief History of Cort Tower

The second skyscraper built in Stockton, the tower was designed by L. B. Dutton and constructed for the Commercial & Savings bank in 1915. With its classic window arches and exquisitely crafted interiors, it exemplifies the Beaux Arts-Renaissance Revival style popular early in the twentieth century.

A fire partially destroyed the structure in 1923. Following the repairs, an additional tower was built and attached to the first, doubling the building's square footage to 100,000 square feet. Over the years there have been several owners, including the Bank of America, the Grupe Company, and American Savings and Loan.

When American took ownership in 1981, the tower  went from being a lovely building to an exquisite one. In the old bank area on the first floor, American established the upscale San Francisco-style Portobello restaurant. On the other floors were credit officers, agents, and loan processors, who were writing loans as fast as they could. Stockton was going through a boom time, and American, this world champion of lenders, was in its halcyon days. Within their opulent offices, complete with oak paneling, huge artisan-painted fireplaces, fourteen-foot doors, elegance from one end to the other, the bank carried on its excessive lending practices.

After the FDIC told American it would have to sell the building, the company was dealt a second blow when the feds required them to render the building totally clean before selling. That meant removing asbestos, repainting, and deep cleaning. These "repairs" were accomplished to the tune of about $1 million on a structure that was already in very good condition. But even with all that, selling it wasn't going to be easy.

American was experiencing the consequences of its own bad practices. For years, they had made high-interest loans and tons of money and were protected by our government, while my friends and neighbors—small business people, or women- or minority-owned businesses—had no such privileges and could never qualify for loans from American. The fact that American was having problems selling their huge building in the environment they helped to create was, to my mind, justice.

Building as the Bank of America is shown in these three photos. Courtesy the Bank of Stockton Historical Photograph Collection.

Choosing a Project:
A Building No One Else Wanted

By the time American Savings and Loan was forced to sell, downtown Stockton could have served as a poster child for the worst effects of urban sprawl. In these depressed surroundings, the bank was attempting to divest itself of a 100,000 square foot beautiful, but impractical, structure. A buyer needed to be able to attract tenants, and filling this huge empty space in an area people had been fleeing for years appeared to be a futile task. It appeared that way to everyone, that is, except me.

The conventional wisdom was that there was no way to draw tenants, but conventional wisdom by definition lacks imagination. By making some practical adjustments and utilizing good marketing tools to inspire a movement back into the area, I believed I could transform the abandoned tower into a desirable business location.

I knew the pressure was on American to sell, and I'd be able to get a tremendous deal. I knew I was the only game in town; no one else was making an offer. I knew that by buying the building at a bargain price, I could give tenants such good rental rates that I'd be able to fill it. In fact, I envisioned the building occupied by all the people that American had shunned—minority-owned businesses, non-profits, accountants, lawyers, marketing people, retail establishments, and others. They would have the opportunity to incubate their enterprises while interacting with others and stimulating economic growth. And they would be doing all this in one of the most beautiful, best-equipped facilities in town.

I also considered the Crosstown Freeway, a marketing tool that I dubbed "The Hundred Million Dollar Cort Tower Tenant Improvement," because the building loomed high above it and could be seen for miles.

Financing: Negotiating the Deal, Rolling the Dice

These combined, positive elements ignited my imagination and my passion to facilitate a transformation in an area where others feared to tread. To the shock of their real estate broker, negotiations began with my offer of $1.1 million. Appalled by the low figure, he assured me American would never accept it. My response was, well, if it does accept, I also want them to rent two floors for the next five years. I really enjoyed his reaction to that, but I meant it. If I could get American to agree, they would be paying approximately $10,000 a month for rent, which could cover the cost of my mortgage and utility bills, and I'd still be making money. It was a nervy offer, but they were desperate to sell and I was the lone bidder.

The agent carried the offer back to Charles Knapp, president of American Savings and Loan in the City of Orange. Knapp didn't like it and sent another big shot, the executive vice president. He came to my office in my Victorian bearing the message that the president didn't want to rent the two floors and wanted to know what I'd offer without the rental stipulation. I said I'd give them $750,000. This wasn't something I had calculated; it just came to me to make that offer, low as it was and outlandish as it seemed. It made sense to me because if they didn't rent the two floors, I was going to have to find other tenants immediately in order to get a loan, and my job would be harder. Again, I took pleasure in the messenger's reaction.

Knapp didn't take to that idea at all, and we agreed on the first offer of $1.1 million with the two-floor rental. But before escrow closed, I decided I was on a roll. This is the exciting part of any negotiation, to take it as far as you can and keep rolling those dice. So I paid a visit to Knapp at his headquarters. It was huge and looked like a rocket ship. I was shown to an office that covered some 15,000 square feet. Now I could see where their investors' money had gone.

Here I was, a thirty-something maverick, showing up at the eleventh hour at the president of American Savings and Loan's office, to pose yet one more option. I recommended to Charlie—we were by that time on a first-name basis—that I pay $1.1 million and his company would rent not only the two floors already discussed, but the entire tower. American's employees still occupied the office building across the street, and I wanted to persuade him that it would be more cost-effective to sell that structure and consolidate all his employees in one location. I also added that if he agreed to go ahead, I'd give him a great deal.

At that point, Charlie may have been tempted to tell me to take my offer and jump off the tenth floor of the tower, but he refrained. He remained convivial, although his reply was an adamant, "No thanks. Absolutely not!" We would stay with the previous deal or there'd be no deal. It was a terrific day of negotiating, and as I flew back to Stockton I couldn't help thinking there was still a chance he'd change his mind.

That call, however, was not forthcoming and it all went through as Knapp wanted. Interest rates were starting to come down, and I got a loan from my favorite bank, the Bank of Stockton. A year after my original offer, we finally closed the deal.

Finding Tenants: Incubating Small Businesses

I set up my company offices on the tenth floor, and my staff and I took great pleasure in the fine amenities and detailed interiors the previous owners had provided. Our presence in the tower was a big selling point. Prospective tenants would see right away that I was on the premises. I'd personally sign the lease. They'd know they could approach me in person any time with whatever problems that came up, and we'd work it out. They would understand soon enough that my intention was to support them in achieving their own visions.

Even though two floors were rented, it was imperative that we bring in more businesses. An almost-empty office building was not an asset. To remedy this, I began dialing for dollars and had my staff do the same. We called every business with an office in Stockton offering them rents they found hard to refuse. We marketed everywhere, every way and to everyone. Our efforts were successful, and my dream was realized. American paved the way for me to load the building with all the tenants they would have turned away.

❐ Naming the Tower: Discovering Its Identifier

What's in a name? In terms of marketing, a lot, and I needed to come up with

the best name for the property. Its identifier, visible from the freeway, had to function as another means of enticing people to check out downtown and the tower. I considered several possibilities until one night in some sort of reverie, it came to me. I'd name it Cort Tower, and not primarily because it was my name. I had an intuition about

Cort Companies executive offices.

this, and I called it Cort Tower because it could be confused with Coit Tower, the famous San Francisco tourist attraction. Stockton is less than two hours from San Francisco, so I thought that I'd send out a subliminal message: tourists in the area visiting the San Joaquin delta might think it's Coit Tower, look again and see it's Cort Tower. The confusion itself was an attention-getting device that I thought would tweak people's interest.

The Cort Tower sign, with its big gold letters, was installed in a style that makes it look like this is its original moniker. It was a different approach to name recognition, but I had a gut feeling it would work.

Design Considerations: On-the-Job Training

Cort Tower turned out to be my master's program in downtown development, a learning experience from the first day. I'd never bought anything in the downtown corridor, and had to learn about every system needed to maintain a 100,000 square foot, ten-story building. Heating, cooling, engineering for high-speed elevators, janitorial services—it was all new to me. Since it was a national historic landmark, there were very specific requirements that needed to be consistently fulfilled.

Also, we were responsible for maintaining the architectural integrity of its original style, and weren't allowed to do much to the exterior of the building. But we had complete leeway on the interior, and even though it was in great condition, I continued to make improvements and did a lot of rebuilding.

One of the first things I constructed was a full-service athletic club on the ground floor. There had never been an athletic club downtown, and I knew there were many potential clients with offices in the area, including city and county workers and other local businesspeople. Today the club has a thousand members, and it's constantly in use. Once again, I had some fun with the name. I called it the Downtown Athletic Club, after the club of the same name in New York that awards the Heisman Trophy each year. I also put a stationery store on the first floor, and built as many kinds of interior spaces as the tenants requested.

❐ Discovering Hidden Architectural Treasure

With every property I buy, there are always moments or events that are magical. One such moment occurred during the construction of the athletic club.

It started with the need for access to the basement. As is often the case with older structures, the original plans for the tower were gone. For a restoration or renovation on a building that's already been through several transformations, there's an element of architectural exploration. In this instance, in tandem with the athletic club facilities being built on the first floor, we were also creating men and women's locker rooms in the basement that were being constructed on opposite sides of the floor. But we only had one stairway going down to the basement in the back, and it opened into the area assigned for the women's locker rooms. This seemed odd. It would have made sense to have had another one in the front because the area was so large.

The men really needed to have a separate entrance. So I told one of my contractors to get a saw, and using our new floor plans, I pointed to the area above the men's locker room that looked to me like the logical place to install another stairway, and asked him to cut out some of the floor. A short time later, the contractor brought me to the hole in the floor and told me to put my hand in it. I did, and felt something made of marble. I told him to keep cutting, and we discovered a gorgeous white marble staircase that went all the way down. It had been hidden behind three walls and was in excellent condition. We just fixed a tread or two and added a beautiful stainless steel bronze railing on top and wood railings going up, and that became the entrance to the men's locker rooms. *Photo shown at right.*

❐ A Very Special Tenant

Here's another bit of magic. One day a woman walked into my office looking to rent space and introduced herself as Margaret Mary Johnston. She mentioned that she was from San Francisco. Something about her was familiar, but I couldn't put my finger on it. I showed her some office space on the eighth floor, and that evening I called my dad to ask him if her name was familiar, thinking that perhaps she was someone I had known in childhood. He did remember her, or more accurately, he remembered her parents. Their family lived across the street from ours when I was growing up. Mary Margaret and I were neighbors; we had probably passed each other on the street more than once. But that wasn't all.

My father related an incident that happened when my mother had been on the television show, "The Price Is Right." I was seven and at home with a babysitter, sick with what everyone thought was a cold. It turned out that I had pneumonia, and that night I passed out. The frantic babysitter called our neighbors from across the street. Mary Margaret's mom, a nurse, came over immediately, and it's very possible that this wonderful woman with her nursing skills saved my life. I had no memory of this.

After I heard the story, I told Mary Margaret that she could make the deal, period! And when her husband ran for state senator, he got an office, too. And that's how it goes.

We all connect and reconnect in mysterious ways. These are some of the ways it happened and continues to happen in Cort Tower, in the central core, the downtown, the great good place. Virtually everyone who rents from me has some kind of story to relate about the place they come to. Every endeavor contains its share of surprises.

Cort Tower is what I've described as a significant identifier. It serves as an impressive, visible example of how transformation can take place. The purpose of creating identifiers is to inspire others to invest in the reutilization of structures in downtown areas, and by doing so, help recreate community. Cort Tower was a building that needed a vision attached to it. There are many others.

❐ Creating and Maintaining A Positive Impression

After completing Cort Tower, I bought, fixed up, and sold The Marketplace, an indoor mall across the street from the Tower. I also purchased some properties on Weber Avenue a couple of blocks away, including the Newbury Building. Then I acquired the Kress building across the street. I had taken similar action with properties near Railroad and Eden Squares.

This is not because I want to own every building in the vicinity. Part of my method is to buy what I refer to as "satellite" buildings and fix them up. I want to enhance the structures surrounding my projects. Ugly, beat-up buildings nearby are aesthetically offensive and bad for business. It is all part of the overriding goal to revitalize the downtown, entice people back, create examples of what can be done to re-enliven a city, and inspire others to invest in Stockton's architectural heritage. If you're tackling a whole area, you may consider this strategy as an additional means of bringing life to it.

There is still a lot of work to be done to achieve a complete turnaround in Stockton. However, there is much more economic activity today than in the early nincties, when we first came on the scene. After dozens of completed projects, Stockton is beginning to appreciate the benefits of having government offices downtown: San Joaquin County's Department of Environmental Health (600 East Main), Office of the Treasurer and Tax Collector (500 East Main, another developer's project), the Family Law Courthouse for the Superior Courts of California, (540 East Main),and the Kress Legal Center and Law Library.

Other additions around town since the early nineties include the baseball stadium; a new movie multiplex; the historic, renovated Fox Theatre Entertainment venue; and the Weber Point Event Center, all connected to the San Joaquin River, a thousand miles of waterways that stretch from Sacramento to San Francisco Bay.

One piece of the puzzle is still missing. The city has not yet grasped the importance of creating residential space downtown. In order for the area to thrive, people have to be living there. I believe that this, too, will come in the near future. There are no shortages of challenges in Stockton, but the turnaround has begun and will continue.

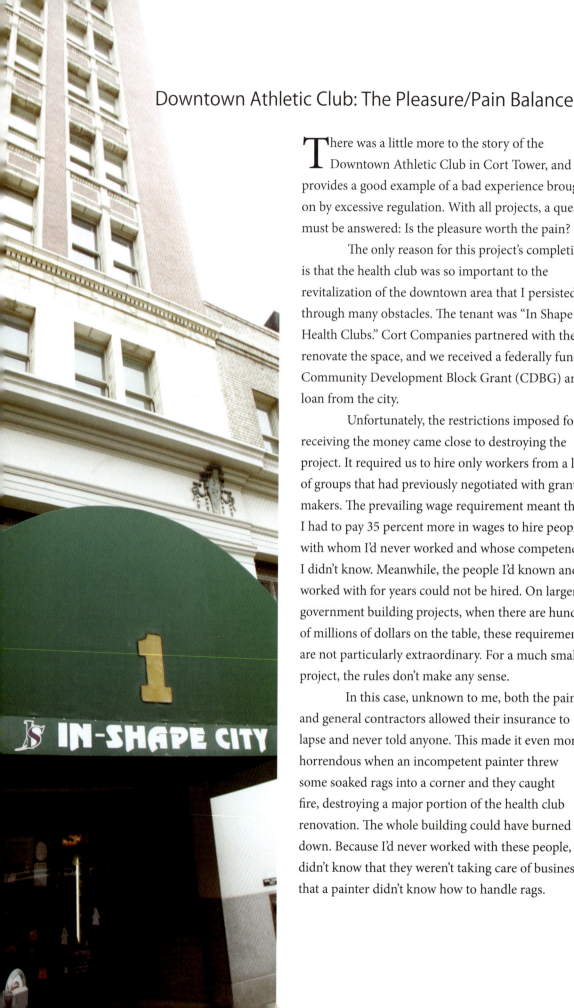

Downtown Athletic Club: The Pleasure/Pain Balance

There was a little more to the story of the Downtown Athletic Club in Cort Tower, and it provides a good example of a bad experience brought on by excessive regulation. With all projects, a question must be answered: Is the pleasure worth the pain?

The only reason for this project's completion is that the health club was so important to the revitalization of the downtown area that I persisted through many obstacles. The tenant was "In Shape Health Clubs." Cort Companies partnered with them to renovate the space, and we received a federally funded Community Development Block Grant (CDBG) and a loan from the city.

Unfortunately, the restrictions imposed for receiving the money came close to destroying the project. It required us to hire only workers from a list of groups that had previously negotiated with grant makers. The prevailing wage requirement meant that I had to pay 35 percent more in wages to hire people with whom I'd never worked and whose competency I didn't know. Meanwhile, the people I'd known and worked with for years could not be hired. On larger government building projects, when there are hundreds of millions of dollars on the table, these requirements are not particularly extraordinary. For a much smaller project, the rules don't make any sense.

In this case, unknown to me, both the painting and general contractors allowed their insurance to lapse and never told anyone. This made it even more horrendous when an incompetent painter threw some soaked rags into a corner and they caught fire, destroying a major portion of the health club renovation. The whole building could have burned down. Because I'd never worked with these people, I didn't know that they weren't taking care of business or that a painter didn't know how to handle rags.

Recovering from this setback was very difficult and added time and expense, but we finally completed the project.

In a situation like this, one might try to find another funding source, but if that source isn't found and the project lies languishing for a long time, that isn't constructive either. A balance has to be found between the strings attached to a project and the need or desire to complete it. Each project is different, and each needs to be considered in all its complexity when accepting funding.

At the time, I knew the club was central to revitalizing the area. It would give people working downtown a place to go to maintain a level of health and to find a sense of belonging. But is the pleasure worth the pain? When you have a beautiful, state-of-the art health club, the first in Stockton's downtown, with a thriving membership, and a few years have passed dimming one's memory, the answer to the question is, of course, yes.

600 and 540 East Main

"Example is not the main thing in influencing others. It is the only thing."
Albert Schweitzer

600 East Main: A Turnaround Begins

The renovation and re-adaptation of 600 East Main Street is a good example of the way a turnaround begins in a downtown neighborhood. When I acquired it, this 50,000 square-foot, early twentieth century structure was an abandoned, water-damaged furniture store. Today it is the home office for San Joaquin County's Department of Environmental Health. Its completion marked the beginning of a renaissance in the east end of Stockton. Several renovations have followed. Today there's new vitality in the area that will continue to expand into the kind of turnaround I believe is possible in all inner-city neighborhoods.

Top, left and facing page: Two views of the entrance and public reception area. Custom design includes open space, tiled floors with diamond pattern, tinted bullet-proof glass, and climate control.

Bottom, left: Original structure as S.F. Floral Co. Courtesy the Bank of Stockton Historical Photograph Collection.

Bottom, facing page: Modern state-of-the art work cubicles, including all office amenities.

540 East Main: Public/Private Partnership at Its Best

The dramatic restoration of 600 East Main Street and its occupancy by the county's Department of Environmental Health paved the way for the next renovation at 540 East Main Street, which has been cited by the State Office of Courts as the result of one of the best public/private partnerships in California. This recognition is especially welcome because creating such solid, mutually beneficial partnerships is one of my major goals.

Constructed in 1890, 540 East Main Street jointly functioned as two hardware stores, Austin Brothers and Hickenbotham Brothers Hardware and Steel. The 90,000 square foot building contains three floors, including the basement. In the 1950s it was renovated and became a J.C. Penney Department Store, which resided there for over thirty years. Purchased by American Savings Bank in the 1980s, it was completely redesigned to accommodate office and bank use. An innovation added by American Savings Bank was an elaborate, automated file storage facility in the basement that could hold millions of records. Washington Mutual later purchased 540 East Main, and then in 2006 decided to sell.

Original condition of the Family Law Courthouse.

Choosing the Project and Finding Tenants

Washington Mutual was asking $3.8 million, which was a very good price considering that it had been recently renovated and well maintained. The modern filing storage system could be a major draw for the right tenant. It happened that at the same time I was considering purchasing the building, the Superior Courts of the State of California were looking for a location for the new Family Law Courthouse for the Superior Courts of California, a fully equipped courtroom building with state-of-the art technology.

Superior courts are county entities, but state people stayed involved. Court officials appraised the qualities and suitability of the building and informed state officials that, with its central location in a downtown parking district and additional parking in the back, 540 East Main Street was a desirable site for a courthouse. A further advantage was that the city of Stockton had finally begun to realize the importance of keeping official buildings downtown.

Facing, top: The Environmental Health Department's occupancy at 600 East encouraged the renovation for the Superior Court at 540 directly across the street. Bottom: J. C. Penny Department Store established in 540 East Main during the 1950s was in residence for over thirty years. Courtesy the Bank of Stockton Historical Photograph Collection.

Below: Built in the early 1900s, 540 East Main had been utilized as a tailor's shop, a dry goods store, a women's clothier, and a real estate office. Courtesy the Bank of Stockton Historical Photograph Collection.

The Domino Effect. Another developer bought the abandoned structure at 500 East Main Street and renovated it.

Cort Companies' recent renovation of 600 East Main Street had a positive impact on the state's decision to work with us. Not only was it an example of a beautiful re-adaptation of a historic building, but its presence in the east end of town, a not-so-desirable neighborhood for many years, asserted that an important government agency had enough confidence in the area to situate its central office there.

All these factors confirmed the suitability of the site for the Superior Court. And who could better utilize an extensive filing storage system than the courts, with their voluminous official documents? I offered to rent them the basement while we built courtrooms on the first and second floors. They accepted.

Today 500 East Main houses the Office of the Treasurer and Tax Collector of San Joaquin County.

Financing the Project

I had recently sold a mixed-use project in Sand City, California to the current tenant. I took the profit from that sale and put it into an IRS 1031 tax-deferred exchange, which is a vehicle for deferring taxes that you trade from one property to another. The 1031 is frequently used in the exchange of like-kind properties. I traded my profit from the Sand City building into this $3.8 million project in Stockton, deferring hundreds of thousands of dollars in taxes.

We crafted leases and collaborated with state architects. The courts agreed to a five-year lease and they got a great deal in rent—significantly below market rates for the first year.

This public/private partnership was also very desirable for the city. It would have cost them about four times more to complete the renovation without my company's involvement. In Lodi, north of Stockton, courtrooms under government auspices were being built for $430 per square foot, and we were offering to build much more quickly at a rate of $110 per square foot. Not an easy deal to pass up.

Design Considerations

Since we were a partnership, there was a lot of collaboration with state and county people in weekly planning meetings. Everything from the type of doors to how big the judges' chambers should be was discussed. The improvements they wanted were very costly, and, of course, we still had to deal with regulations. For example, to satisfy the seismic retrofitting requirements, we had to install chevron steel bracing, a stipulation more likely to be found in San Francisco than in Stockton. We built fire corridors and made numerous other improvements.

Inside the court building, we combined clean lines and modern design and utilized high-tech materials, such as stainless steel for seating and reinforced glass as cubicle dividers. In addition, we incorporated artwork from the community through a partnership with the local schools. A contest was held, the winners of which would have their paintings framed and hung in the Superior Court building. These paintings represent the inclusion of children and community within a government facility that happens to be transacting matters of family law.

We completed the conversion and the building was occupied within eight months. The final result is dramatic. It's as if the building has been transported in a time machine from the late nineteenth century to the twenty-first. Its architecture is modern and elegant, and it possesses all the amenities of the latest technology—special security systems, high speed Internet, data lines and custom insulation. The highest level of acoustic engineering provides soundproofing for each courtroom. It's virtually impossible for anyone outside a courtroom to hear whatever exchanges are transpiring within. All the architectural and technological renovations were done to accommodate the needs of the court.

Combining modern design within an older structure is what I do in all my projects, with excellent results. Rather than conflicting with each other, the old and the new, when incorporated with good taste and good sense, coexist elegantly. This is also true of historic and modern buildings existing side by side. One style does not preclude the other, and often the juxtapositions are visually stimulating and lively. Variety creates a sense of place within older downtowns.

Superior Courts' first floor reception area for the public with built-in lower surfaces to accommodate handicap access.

Following page: State-of-the-art courtroom possesses all the amenities of the latest technology - security systems, data lines, custom insulation and engineered soundproofing.

Above: Another courtroom view displaying the witness box and the elegant simplicity of the design. Facing page: Waiting area with modern seating design. Paintings are by students from local schools who participated in a contest.

Public/Private Partnerships: Win/Win

I've stated several times that one of my primary objectives is to improve communication and create partnerships between the private and government sectors. In that regard, this project was especially gratifying. In the case of 540 East Main Street, Cort Companies worked with both county and state government agencies on every aspect of renovation from the planning stages to completion of the project. Through these partnerships, the agencies got to see firsthand the gritty realities and complex challenges with which a historic building restorer contends. They also had to abide by governmental restrictions imposed on a restoration. If government agencies can see how their rules help or impede progress, they may see their way to changing some of the more excessive regulations.

The success of these two partnerships inspires hope for mutually beneficial affiliations to become more common. When an experienced private sector contractor cooperates with a public entity that understands and appreciates its contributions to economic health, everyone wins.

The proof is that our work there isn't finished. We've been contracted to add three more courtrooms on the second floor, and that project may well be expanded.

The Domino Effect

Creating the new courthouse was an opportunity to continue revitalization in the east end of town, which until the restoration of 600 East Main had been the most rundown area of the city. And renovation has a domino effect. The reinvigorated 600 and 540 East Main Street buildings anchor two of the four corners at American and Main streets. Other developers have also contributed to the area's revitalization. At 500 East Main, one bought the dilapidated structure that it is now the office of the Treasurer and Tax Collector of San Joaquin County.

An architect from Santa Barbara bought the old Terry Hotel across from the courthouse and plans to build retail space and a food court. More recently, the North Shore Waterfront Baseball Stadium was built as well as the Events Center and the new Sheraton Hotel, all in close proximity to the new court building. This is healthy growth.

The east end of Stockton is now filled with people dashing to offices, restaurants or baseball games. There's new life in the area. To complete the turnaround, the next step the city must undertake is to create residential districts so that people can make their homes in the neighborhood. Even without that, it's still about the safest area of town with access to the stadium, theaters, offices, farmers markets, and the great San Joaquin River.

The Kress Legal Center and Law Library

"Interiors change radically while exteriors maintain continuity. The space plan is the stage of the human comedy. New scene, new set."
Stewart Brand, *How Buildings Learn*

From Abandoned Building to Regional Landmark

The S. H. Kress building in downtown Stockton had been empty for years when I acquired it in 2003. Although it was a significant, historic structure, it had languished because no one had figured out how to convert it into an economically viable venture. The potential was there for an exquisite restoration that would contribute to the revitalization of the area, but a new owner had to be willing to deal with unreasonable, costly government regulations; find trustworthy, respectable, long-term tenants; and form new partnerships as well as rely on established ones for financing and other requirements.

This chapter tells the story of how this abandoned building was transformed into the flourishing Kress Legal Center and Law Library, and recognized as a regional landmark. For this renovation I was presented in 2006 with the prestigious Glenn Allen Award for excellence in restoration from the Stockton Cultural Heritage Board.

Brief History of S. H. Kress

The S. H. Kress building was constructed in 1930 as one of a chain of five-and-dime retail stores originated by Samuel H. Kress. His company built over 250 of these establishments in twenty-nine states between 1896 and 1955. The Kress stores carried everything: sewing kits, clothing, toys, Halloween masks, make-up, and cleaning and hardware supplies, all at prices that most everyone could afford. The merchandise was displayed in rows from one end of the floor to the other. Each store featured a soda fountain where one could find refreshment with a cup of coffee, a sandwich, or an ice cream soda. The Stockton fountain had a reputation for the best cheesecake in town. As a meeting place, it was the site of many a first date and a few marriage proposals.

The way Kress stores were managed represented old American values. They were honored to serve the public and proud to sell items made in America and made to last. Because they respected their employees and wanted a happy working and shopping environment, many people worked at Kress their entire careers, forming lifelong relationships. Their salaries were enough to cover the cost of living in Stockton.

The congenial store atmosphere was reflected in the special attention bestowed on the architecture of the buildings. Samuel Kress was an art collector, and he took pride in creating beautiful structures, originally distinguished by yellow brick and terra cotta façades. His architectural inspirations derived from

Popular soda fountain in all Kress stores.

Facing page: S.H. Kress building in 1928. Courtesy the Bank of Stockton Historical Photograph Collection.

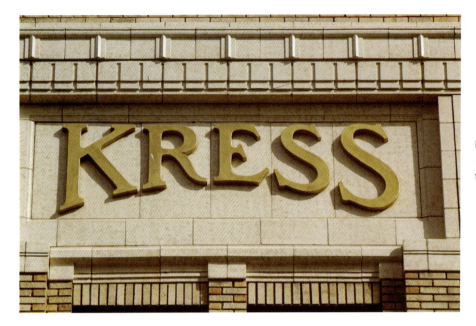

Kress structures were originally distinguished by yellow brick and terra cotta facades.

classical Greek and Italian Renaissance structures. Each was unique, constructed with sensitivity to the surrounding environment, but its identifier, the Kress logo, was always prominently displayed in elegant lettering.

Around 1929, the stores were redesigned in the simpler, more modern art deco mode, which is the architectural style of the Stockton store. Many Kress stores still stand, and, like this one, have been adaptively renovated for present-day use. The company's history and designs are preserved in the book, *America's 5 & 10 Cent Stores: The Kress Legacy* by Bernice L. Thomas, which displays and discusses the Stockton building. This wonderful book was a gift from our first tenant in the renovated Kress.

The Kress logo was always prominently displayed in elegant lettering.

After the original business closed, and the building had gone unused, a San Francisco company bought it with the intention of recreating the old five-and-dime environment and ambiance. But times had changed and, to the disappointment of its new owners, that type of store had become obsolete. It was unable to compete in an economy of flourishing big-box stores that carried the same items for lower prices. The business closed in 1992.

By the time I purchased the building in late 2003, I had a pretty strong track record for downtown architectural restorations. Over the years, I'd developed important business affiliations with lenders, city and county officials, the private and public sectors, as well as architects, designers, and contractors. I'd established a reputation and had proven to my creditors that I was reliable. My own team at Cort

Companies had been together over a decade. We were, and remain, a tight-knit group. Everyone is cross-trained and can be depended upon to play a variety of roles.

My purpose in highlighting these relationships is to emphasize that the success of a project depends on the strength of associations and partnerships developed over time. Anyone interested in pursuing this kind of work must, from the beginning, cultivate supportive business relationships while establishing a positive track record. The Kress project is a good example of partnerships in action.

Choosing a Project: The Lure and Lore of the Kress

There were many good reasons to consider buying the Kress. First, Mahala Burns, my real estate broker, (I call her my muse because of her amazing intuition about such things) had been urging me to buy the building for a long time. That in itself was an inducement to make the purchase, and there were others. The four-story building, constructed of high-quality materials, with its exquisite art deco façade and beautiful maple floors, offered numerous creative opportunities for interior architectural construction. Another substantial motivation was its location, directly across the street from Cort Tower. An abandoned building in disrepair did nothing to support my goal of a revitalized downtown. Finally, as I mentioned, the Kress held a special place in the hearts of Stocktonians.

Another enticement was the price: $650,000–although it's important to bear in mind that a low price tag usually suggests that no one has figured out how to make a return on an investment. It would only be worth the price if I could transform it into a desirable, profitable business center.

I put Mahala in charge of doing what she does best: coming up with the essential element without which the project would be untenable—that is, finding reliable, long-term tenants.

Finding Tenants

A series of synchronicities culminated in a terrific mix of tenants. Two prominent attorneys, one the president of the Bar Association of San Joaquin County and his wife, an expert in international law, were the first people interested in renting space at the Kress. They were so taken with beauty of the architecture that they were willing to wait over a year for the restoration to be completed. They even leased an office across the street in order to keep an eye on the construction and progress of "their" suite. The beautiful book mentioned above on the Kress legacy was a gift from them.

The bar president used his influence to persuade the association to rent the entire third floor. Eventually, the second floor was inhabited by his firm, his wife's office, and several other private law firms. Mahala had also found a law firm interested in renting the fourth floor, an area more like a penthouse and much smaller than the other floors. All our future tenants were amenable to long-term leases, a necessity if I was going to get the financing I needed.

Knowing I could occupy three of the four floors, and confident that Mahala would be able to find a first-floor tenant, I went ahead and bought the building. My confidence was soon rewarded. Mahala found a first-floor occupant that would provide an impressive anchor for the enterprise and stimulate a beautiful reconstruction.

Unique architectural enhancements throughout.

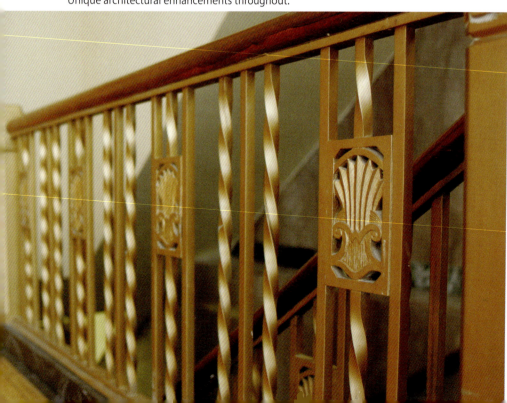

The law library on the first floor was the most exciting of the renovations.

Public/Private Partnerships

At the time there was a county reorganization going on. Part of the plan involved the courthouse, which had been deemed inadequate to meet county needs. It was destined for demolition, and its occupants would eventually be compelled to find new space. It happened that the San Joaquin County Law Library, which had been located in the courthouse for years, had wanted to expand and, with the impending loss of their space, was ready to make a change. Mahala thought that the first floor of the Kress, in the heart of the developing downtown city/county office corridor, would be a perfect site for the library.

I liked that idea a lot. I could foresee building a mezzanine and crafting unique architectural enhancements that would create a stunning library space. In addition, the library was agreeable to a long-term lease.

Building lobby and entrance to the San Joaquin County Law Library.

Financing

By 2003, I was well acquainted with the hidden financial burdens a project can present. And once again, I had to find financial support outside the city, this time from Monterey County Bank who, along with several other regional banks, has become a strong supporter of my vision. Their officers not only believe that what I do is valuable, but they also understand the unique challenges of historic buildings. It's ironic that the Stockton Cultural Heritage Board will present a plaque to hang on a wall, but none of the city's institutions will provide financing. Although they're pleased when a renovation is complete, they would rather put their money elsewhere than invest in the heart and soul of their own city.

Obviously with any financing, loan conditions are important. A fixed-rate loan with as small a payment as possible over the longest period of time is most desirable. However, equally important to negotiating a manageable loan is knowing that the lender really gets what you're trying to do—and the challenges you face doing it. The surprises old buildings present—the floor that isn't level and needs to be replaced; the leak that's destroyed an entire wall; the systems that, while made out of high-quality materials, are now obsolete—must always be factored into the estimated investment. If your bank understands this and sees a good track record in your payments and in your tenants, you're way ahead of the game.

In this case, the price of the building was low, but the investment was going to be high. This was due not only to the cost for designers, contractors, and building materials, but also to the high expense of satisfying government regulations.

Design Considerations

Like all restoration projects, Kress presented its unique brand of structural and creative challenges. Except for the wall facing the street, there were virtually no windows, just brick walls on the north and east sides and a few windows at the top of the south side. As a five-and-dime, only the first floor had been used for commerce, and the basement for the soda fountain. The second, third, and fourth floors

were utilized to manufacture boxes, and as warehouse space. A machine made of cast iron, bigger than a truck and weighing several tons, filled the second floor. Its purpose had been to break down boxes, assemble packaging, and wrap sold items. It was quite a production to dismantle and remove it in parts. There were also changing areas for employees. Since they had been utilized mainly for industrial purposes and were not seen by the public, the interiors were minimal and rough.

To illuminate the dark interior, we rewired the entire building to get as much power and lighting as possible. Big, modern, Italian-style fluorescent lights added style and were economical as well. We cut into the brick and created windows on the whole north side. We built handicap-accessible restrooms, which required major plumbing adjustments, lowered thresholds, and widened doors to accommodate wheelchairs. The building had to be retrofitted, and asbestos and lead paint removed. New mechanical systems had to be installed.

The law library on the first floor was the most exciting of the renovations. Complex railing designs and mezzanines were built overlooking study areas. Open industrial, loft-like spaces, and a large area for bookshelves created a comfortable, expansive, user-friendly environment. We redid the maple floors and added handsome carpets that complement the rich color of the wood.

Since it was all wide-open space on the three floors above, each tenant could specify the kind of space they wanted. If someone wanted a wall, we put up a wall. The fourth floor was fashioned to have the look of a New York Fifth Avenue office. An elevator opened into the company lobby from which could be seen glass enclosures for workplaces. Essentially, each business was able to custom design their office space for a fraction of what they would pay for a non-custom office in another building.

When the major restorations were complete, we hired Rusty Buckingham, a world-famous muralist from New York, to paint the large lobby wall. His art deco rendering of Blind Justice holding the legal scales is the striking image seen immediately upon entering the library. It's a strong statement and an impressive sight. A little-known secret is that the face of Blind Justice and Mahala's visage are quite similar. This is because Mahala, Rusty's sister, posed for the project. We like to keep things in the family.

Today, my tenth floor office in Cort Tower overlooks the Kress Legal Center and Law Library, one more contribution that embodies our commitment to the revitalization of downtown Stockton. These projects demand dedication, time, attention, money, and patience. One begins with a vision for a better environment. With the right people and partnerships—public/private; landlord/tenant; lender/borrower; visionary/architect; past/present—that vision can be manifested.

The Monterey Peninsula

"There's a reason that Elm Street and Main Street resonate in our cultural memory. It's not because we're sentimental saps. It's because this pattern of human ecology produced places that worked wonderfully well, and which people deeply loved."

James Howard Kunstler

Relocating to Pacific Grove

I have been a permanent resident of the Monterey Peninsula, more specifically Pacific Grove (PG), since 1996. After living in Stockton on and off for over twenty five years, I was ready to live in an environment with proximity to the coast more like the one in which I'd grown up, and I was seeking a lifestyle one finds in a smaller community. I was not giving up on Stockton or its turnaround. I never have; I remain involved as ever. The idea was to do most of my business on the computer and by phone, but to be within a few hours' driving distance of my company office in Stockton and available to go in as needed.

In 1994, I began checking out a lot of different places in which I might settle. The Monterey Peninsula is an idyllic central coast area containing many of the elements I sought. When I investigated further, the small coastal town of Pacific Grove seemed the perfect setting for my family and me. It's a beautiful place with a gentle climate built on a human scale and, coincidentally, is endowed with more Victorian houses per capita than anywhere else in America. The Victorians and other historic architecture date back to the late 1800s. The Monterey Bay Aquarium, a terrific museum of natural history, and a famous butterfly sanctuary where clouds of monarch butterflies gather from October to February contribute to PG's unique character. It's a small, safe

Left: Victorian shops downtown Pacific Grove.

Facing page: Butterfly Habitat, Pacfic Grove.

community in which it's easy to get involved.

I found a house perfectly situated for my family, but the structure itself was a train wreck; it had asbestos siding, poor plumbing, poor orientation, and a mudroom blocking the ocean view. I bought it, then rented it out for two years while I dealt with the complexities of acquiring coastal commission and building permits that would allow me to renovate the structure. When we finally moved in, I took it apart and rebuilt it. My five-year old son donned a hardhat and a small sledge hammer and gleefully helped me demolish this beat-up old, 1970s ranch-style house. We took down the mudroom and most of the other walls, and finally could see the ocean. For the first couple of years I commuted to Stockton regularly, but eventually settled into living in PG full time, running the business from home except for occasional trips to the office.

Living on the Monterey Peninsula has enabled me to take on a few projects in the area, one in Pacific Grove itself and a couple in the West End of Sand City.

A Brief History of Pacific Grove

Pacific Grove began in 1875 as a Methodist retreat camp. Inspired by the peaceful setting, worshippers gathered here in the summer months. Whole families camped in rough tents. After a couple of years the location became part of a nationwide educational/cultural network. Permanent residences were built, but for quite a while they were inhabited only in the summer. In 1889 the retreat center was incorporated and the city was born.

Eventually others moved to town. Chinese immigrants settled in a small fishing village, and Chinese workers built a lot of the infrastructure in the emerging town. Today, PG is a town of about 16,000 residents and is situated over two square miles.

Lovers Point.

Central and 7th: Tenants In Common, Another Approach to Revitalization

A few years ago, my wife and I were looking for an affordable way for members of our families to enjoy our hometown of Pacific Grove together by creating a family compound of some sort. We bought a rundown apartment building with seven units on Central and Seventh streets. Our plan was to create a Tenants In Common (TIC) partnership, which is a less well-known option than a condominium conversion, but has several advantages.

One of the major distinctions between the two is that parking requirements are less stringent with a TIC, because you are buying the property as it exists in its current condition without the burden of having to build or create something new. If the property has parking units then they are included in the purchase, but there is no requirement to add spaces. With a condominium, there are specific guidelines regarding parking and other provisions that usually demand new construction and added expense. The TIC offers greater flexibility for owners and is in step with an era in which automobile use will, of necessity, become more limited.

TICs are not new—I mentioned a similar arrangement in the chapter on Victorians—but they're more common on the East Coast and in large cities. They are less familiar to real estate professionals and individuals in smaller communities in America. As people begin to appreciate the financial advantages of TICs and the variety of ways they can be utilized, they will become an increasingly attractive choice for co-ownership.

The building we purchased was in terrible condition and so was relatively cheap. It was one of those structures you find even in affluent towns that was bought for thirty or forty thousand dollars decades ago and is still inhabited by some of the original tenants paying the original rents of a couple hundred dollars a month. In exchange for the low rents, the units have had little maintenance. In this case, the building's sagging decks, leaking roof, and moldy walls were dangerous, not to mention health hazards.

We gave the long-time tenants a significant amount of time to find replacement housing before we started construction. When the building was vacated, we discovered that severe drainage problems had caused the mold. We tore out everything from the foundations in the streets and sidewalks to the roof and the walls. We completely rebuilt it with top quality materials and installed state-of-the-art improvements.

It's a beautiful renovation perfect for a family compound. Unfortunately, after it was completed, circumstances changed for various family members, making participation impossible. As it turns out, my wife and I kept a unit, and another was purchased by a retiring facilities manager from my company. The other units have sold.

TICs are perfect contra-developer material: partner with others and buy a large unit that's not in particularly good condition for a relatively low price and then, using as much sweat equity as possible, renovate it based on the needs of the partners. With the proper zoning, one could create affordable workforce housing or collaborate with fellow professionals and have a storefront on the first floor and living units above. One or more of these restorations in a homogeneous community has the potential to usher in a new diversity of people of all ages, professions, and incomes, thereby revitalizing an entire area.

Sand City and West End: A Sleepy Town Transforms Itself

Sand City is a small bohemian town of a couple hundred residents fronting the Pacific Ocean and bordering Seaside and Monterey. Originally an industrial town with large warehouse and factory spaces, it became the site for big-box stores, hosting Target, Costco, Office Depot, and other chains. Street activity was practically nonexistent. The only reasons to be in the vicinity were because one worked there or was seeking professional services from one of the resident businesses.

In 2000 when my wife and I considered buying a building in Sand City, many artists and sculptors had discovered the little town as a peaceful and inexpensive place to rent and create their art. Several had transformed rundown buildings or lofts into stunning studios and live/work spaces. Many other homes, however, were in ramshackle condition.

Choosing the Project

For decades, Couroc, a longstanding company covering nearly a full block on Contra Costa Street in Sand City, manufactured decorative plastic plates with pressed images, including school insignias, historic sights such as San Francisco cable cars, and flower arrangements accented with gold leaf, colorful schemes, and alabaster finishes. In the thirties and forties, Couroc plates adorned many kitchens and living rooms across the country.

But by 2000 the company could no longer compete with inexpensive Chinese labor and was closing its doors. The owner wanted to sell quickly and was offering a good deal: $450,000 for the building, which sat on approximately 15,000 square feet—about a third of an acre. The structure itself, filled with huge iron, obsolete machinery, wasn't worth much, but its location close to the ocean made it valuable. It was an intriguing prospect, but because of other commitments at the time, I decided not to buy.

A year later the owners contacted me again and offered to sell for about $350,000. Before I agreed, I had exhaustive studies done on the soil to determine whether it had been affected by any of Couroc's plastic waste. The results showed that the plastic had been disposed of systematically and properly, and there was no residual pollution. That was good news.

Sand City seemed ready to transform itself from an industrial hub into a center of community activity with new housing units, meeting places, and local retail. The building was located off the bike path that runs from Pacific Grove through Monterey and Sand City to Marina. If an attraction of some kind were installed at the site of the old Couroc factory, it would be an invitation to cyclists and pedestrians on the path to stop there and explore the town.

Sand City was ready to change its image and I recognized its potential. There was already some movement toward reinvention, but like many places with good intentions, it needed some help transitioning from discussion into construction.

I agreed to purchase the factory. The building needed an identifier, so I renamed it "West End." That simple change created a new and different ambiance for the town. With my designer and friend, Michelle Manos, we developed a graphic that resembled the architecture and feel of Cannery Row. That was the concept: then came the work.

The Monterey Peninsula 167

Design Considerations

There was a lot of cleanup. Literally tons of huge machinery had to be removed. I spent tens of thousands of dollars cleaning the concrete floor and having the plastic refuse carted away by certified waste specialists. Then I removed the entire shell—its roof and four walls—leaving only the concrete floor and the steel frame, just the bones. We re-skinned the building with corrugated metal, installed handsome glass rollup doors and copper light fixtures, and tiled walkways outside. Inside it was mainly open space. The project modeled a back-to-the-future design, adding a historic flavor to that part of town.

Finding Tenants

My first tenant was the owner of a tile shop. Then the Ol' Factory, a large café/restaurant, took up residence next to the shop. The tile shop remains and the café became a center for political discourse, performance, and community events. The café owner continued the theme of sustainability and green building on the interior space by using low-chemical paints, eucalyptus and recycled woods, and waterless urinals. When other individuals, like the café owner, carry on the principles of sustainability and community, contra-developers know their work has been successful.

Eventually, the owner of the tile shop decided to buy the building, which signaled his commitment to the revitalization of the town.

Because Sand City has been home to many creative people in various disciplines, we began an annual festival called "West End Celebration." Once a year, artists and artisans roll up the doors to their studios and display their work. Live music, dance, and street performance, as well as ethnic food vendors, spill into the streets. The festival has been extremely successful and continues to affirm a sense of community.

The Turnaround

I purchased and renovated one other modest building in the area to further support the momentum toward revitalization. The turnaround has begun, and now it's up to the people in the arts, retail, and food industries to continue to infill in Sand City to keep the ball rolling. The town is committed to creating a more vibrant community and making the area more pedestrian-friendly, attractive, and accessible. My long-term vision for this area is to be able to drive to the entrance of Sand City, park the car, and walk to the beach through a tunnel/walkway that one day will be built under the freeway. There would be vendors lining the walkway and people on the beach swimming or throwing a Frisbee. It would be an ideal spot to relax and have fun.

Even without the tunnel, the introduction of The West End has perpetuated big changes, enhancing the town's image and ushering in new vitality and energy. Sand City's official website defines itself today as "… a green conscious and artistic community that lives, works, and plays by the sea. Residents and tourists alike enjoy biking through town or spending the day shopping and visiting one of the local eateries, artists' studios or magnificent coastal amenities."

It has come a long way in less than ten years.

Historic City Hall at Forest and Laurel Avenues, recently renovated.

The Office of Mayor

When I bought my house, the farthest thought from my mind was that one day I'd be Mayor of Pacific Grove. However, my San Francisco upbringing, the island experiment in sustainable living, and my career restoring historic inner-city buildings combined to be highly suitable preparation for the position.

As mayor, I had an opportunity to catalyze a turnaround in one small city by applying the principles I've come to believe in over the years. Having a leadership and policymaking role allowed me to encourage constructive partnerships and confront the impediments of specific government rules and regulations. And, most importantly, I was able to work with the community toward making PG a model of urban growth and a green, self-sustaining city.

This section will outline my civic involvement and illustrate a number of ways that you might serve your community as a citizen and entrepreneur.

As I reflect on it now, my life on Darrah's island so many years ago provided the foundation for my activities as mayor of Pacific Grove. Just as growing up in San Francisco gave me a deep appreciation for cities, the island experience provided me with the confidence to create a self-sustaining environment with others. Utilizing the resources of the land and river, finding creative ways to solve problems, and working in partnership provided the apprenticeship for my current position.

As the decades passed and sprawl covered the countryside like a bad rash, I knew the time would come when, in order to survive, people would have to return to a way of life similar to ours on the island, with one big difference: we would have to become sustainable in our cities, towns and neighborhoods, not on our separate islands or outlying suburbs.

As mayor of a small city, I had the opportunity to apply what I learned and work in partnership with the residents of Pacific Grove to form a green, sustainable environment.

The Red House Café on Lighthouse Avenue is an excellent example of utilizing historic architecture.

Civic Action

I did not choose to be mayor, at least not initially. I did choose, however, to do what I believe we all should do: become involved in the community. I applied to be on the planning commission and was appointed by the mayor. Eventually, I chaired the commission. The historic architecture in PG had great potential to be utilized more effectively, and I wanted to see it happen.

My seat on the planning commission gave me an excellent vantage point from which to view PG politics. As a preservationist and contra-developer, I was interested in seeing architecture restored rather than building new. I also wanted to encourage a connection between the larger community and the local government.

After a while on the commission, it became clear that if I wanted to make significant changes, it would have to be by developing policy. So I ran for the city council on a platform that emphasized planning for the future and creating a green, sustainable environment. I talked about the need to save our urban forest by planting trees, the goal never to have another sewer leak (there had been one before I took office that resulted in a million-dollar lawsuit against the town), and the necessity to rebuild downtown and revitalize the local economy.

I won the seat on the council and shortly thereafter, the mayor assigned me the position of vice-mayor. Within a year, he became ill and left office, and the council appointed me mayor. I felt the job fit, and have since run for the position twice and was reelected.

Gosby House Bed & Breakfast on Lighthouse Avenue.

Downtown Turnaround for Pacific Grove

Before I took office, Pacific Grove faced many of the same challenges other communities encounter.

- ❐ The city had to learn to live within its means.
- ❐ The city needs to utilize its natural and built resources more efficiently, seek alternative energy sources and a greener, self-sustaining lifestyle.
- ❐ Some historic architecture isn't well utilized and should be repurposed by creating mixed-use spaces to stimulate the economy.
- ❐ New building should happen through infill and building up, not out. (Fortunately, building out Stockton-style is not an option because of PG's limited land mass.)
- ❐ More residents need to be enticed into the town center.
- ❐ Small businesses should be encouraged and supported, and partnerships, including public/private partnerships, must be strengthened.
- ❐ Finally, more citizens need to become involved in creating and maintaining a healthy community.

For an effective turnaround, all the items above must come together to optimize potential and create the green, sustainable, healthy eco-tourist location PG can be. Accomplishing this is a complicated, sometimes daunting, task, but while I was mayor, each one was addressed and is in a stage of development. The following pages describe how I approached the multiple challenges of that office with the ultimate goal of renewing, revitalizing, and greening this beautiful city.

When I transitioned from being on the city planning commission to becoming mayor, I was in a good position to make some of the changes, together with the city council, that I thought necessary. The first couple of years in office were devoted to balancing a budget that was way out of whack. Employees had been hired that the city couldn't afford; we had a California Public Employment Retirement System (CALPERS) that was too expensive. We eliminated 35 percent of all employees making over $100,000 a year, and balanced a budget that had been experiencing a $2.5 million deficit.

Unfortunately, in the process, services were cut back, including library hours. We recently passed a tax bill that will restore some of those services, and received a grant from the Packard Foundation for $250,000 for the operations of the natural history museum.

Of course, balancing a budget is an ongoing process. In today's challenging economy, there is a tendency to seek economic solutions that are not really solutions in the long run. Within most American cities, there is a lot of contentious discussion about how to handle fiscal problems. I still maintain that the crisis we face is the result of bad planning and the only way to turn it around is with good long-term planning and applying the principles I've discussed in this book. Seeking quick-fix solutions is the worst thing we can do.

Downtown farmers market.

The Monterey Bay Aquarium, housed in historic Hovden's Cannery on Cannery Row.

❐ Utilizing Built Resources

I applied my experience working in downtown redevelopment and restoring properties to assisting property owners in making the most out of PG's built environment. I was able to help them understand the many ways buildings could be renovated and the benefits of readapting an old structure into one that is more utilitarian, stronger, seismically engineered, and accessible. An example of this is our renovation of an old apartment building on Seventh and Central, which is discussed earlier in this chapter.

In order for Pacific Grove to become a prosperous, self-sustaining entity, constructive building ventures must take place. For this to happen, a connection needs to be established between property owners and community development advocates. The city government must communicate to owners, developers, and citizens that all their ideas are welcome and that city officials will listen.

Facing page: Mixed-use Victorians, residential and commercial, Pacific Grove.

There is some terrific historic architecture in town from government buildings to homes to old stores. The old Holman's department store building, pictured at left, is a perfect example. Constructed in 1924, it was once an all-purpose department store that covered a city block; it now houses an antique store on the first floor, and the upper floors are underutilized. It would be great to see this grand old building restored and new units built on the upper floors to serve as lofts or apartments that would provide housing to businesspeople with commercial spaces nearby. This would be a return to the longtime tradition I advocate when people could walk to work from their homes and had time to enjoy their lives. There are spaces that could be adding to PG's general and financial well-being, but are languishing. I hoped to facilitate new ways to think about old properties while bringing awareness to the economic advantages that accompany historic restoration, including stimulus for local businesses, tax credits and significant cost benefits derived from the Mills Act.

An example of the type of renovation I advocated in PG took place a few years ago when a retired woman who loved to dance bought an office building on 17th Street that was dark and filled with small cubicles. She transformed it into a beautiful, light-filled, successful dance studio called Shall We Dance.

This restoration had a domino effect that benefited an entire community educationally, artistically, and economically. It's a terrific example of the kind of restoration that PG should be supporting in every way possible.

Facing page: Butterfly Habitat, Pacfic Grove.

❒ Utilizing Natural Resources

With its location on the Pacific coast, PG is rich in resources that must be cared for and cultivated. A couple of years ago, my wife and I started "Trees for PG," an urban reforestation project. With groups of volunteers, we planted two thousand tree seedlings and saplings in and around Washington Park and throughout Pacific Grove. We raised $30,000 through donations and grants. We planted trees and put in a drip irrigation system in our world-famous butterfly sanctuary. Projects like these are fun, contribute to the greater good, and build community through volunteer efforts. Grants from Pacific Gas & Electric and other sources helped sponsor "Trees for PG." We also installed a bronze tree of life on a wall inside City Hall, and when someone donates money for a sapling, his or her name is engraved on a plaque and placed on the tree.

"Sustainable Pacific Grove," whose mission is to "make Pacific Grove a model of transition to sustainability through innovative, active, and local solutions that enhance community," began under our leadership. It's a volunteer organization, and its website provides information on what's been done and what still needs to be done in PG to make it self-sustaining. Keeping the vision in the forefront of people's minds through educational talks, events, and media is primary. "Sustainable PG" is a strong model for volunteer participation that other cities can follow.

Pacific Grove was one of the first cities in Monterey County to ban the use of Styrofoam take-out containers (a major ocean polluter). We began to develop a model of a green building code similar to that of our neighbor, Monterey. This included using recycled building materials containing less toxic material, utilizing solar panels when possible, and recapturing gray water for lawns. PG was also the first city in Monterey County to sign the United Nations Urban Environmental Accords, which identify ways cities can become more sustainable, and the U.S. Mayors Climate Protection Agreement, which pledges to meet or exceed the Kyoto Protocol's carbon emission target.

Partnerships: Making Things Happen in the Built and Natural Environments

Just as I have had to gather a team of architects, lawyers, contractors, and administrators for successful renovations, the same held true for successful ventures for PG. One of my primary objectives as mayor was to encourage collaborations, including public/private partnerships. As mayor, I was on the public side of these relationships, but I called upon my private business experience to educate the community on how to approach problems imaginatively and to create positive affiliations that may not have been considered in the past.

❐ Water Source and Partnerships

A good example of creative partnerships in action—and one I'm particularly happy about—revolved around discovering a potential water resource for PG. Ironically, this water source was utilized for decades but later abandoned and forgotten. California American Water Company (Cal Am) took over the control of water, and the reservoir built into the side of a hill in 1897 by 1,500 Chinese immigrants. When it was built, water from Carmel Valley, the Carmel River, and other sources was captured and pumped into that reservoir, providing PG with all the non-potable water it needed.

For years no one's given it a thought. Cal Am has been using it as a corporation storage yard. I looked at it one day, and it came to me that here was the water source for the future of PG. I put together a coalition of property owners, environmentalists, and elected officials to see if we could cobble together a plan to use the reservoir. Getting it into operation again would be a giant step toward PG's sustainability.

The Packard Foundation, a longtime supporter of the aquarium and an environmental leader, gave us a grant of $45,000 for the first phase of engineering, which has been completed. I received a mandate from the council for another $45,000 for the second engineering phase. The Foundation knew PG needed water and that the water filling this reservoir was going to come from storm water runoff, and wouldn't pollute our bay. Further, it will be used to maintain our golf courses (a source of income), parks, and other outdoor environments. These improvements key directly into Packard's environmental protection philosophy. It is a perfect public/private partnership.

Right now PG's golf courses are being watered with potable water that is costing the city about $480,000 a year. Cal Am is making adjustments because of our limited water source

Pacific Grove Municipal Golf Course near Point Pinos Lighthouse on the tip of the Monterey Peninsula.

and it could triple the cost for PG up to $1.3 million a year. In addition, if the golf courses did go brown because we couldn't afford to water them, PG would to lose some 90,000 rounds of golf a year, which is millions of dollars of income. This is why the reservoir project must be completed.

Several partnerships are involved in this significant project. I negotiated with Cal Am with the hope that it would donate the property once the City got the rest of the financing. This would be a public/private partnership between the city and the private company, Cal Am. The Packard Foundation also is a private partner. Through another partnership, in the form of a grant from the federal government, we were able to get interns from the Monterey Institute of International Studies to write grants for the reservoir and other projects for $5 an hour, with a balance of $20 paid through the grant. Interns get a total of $25 and we get their services for five. Not a bad deal.

❐ Power Purchase Agreement Partnerships

Part of becoming sustainable is having a power source that will protect PG from rate increases from Pacific Gas & Electric Company. That source is solar power, which will reduce or remove its carbon footprint and make it an environmentally sound town. In as little as seven years, PG wouldn't have an electric bill; it would be generating its own power through solar collectors on our buildings. To do that I wanted to initiate a power purchase agreement.

The way that works is a city official goes to an investor and asks him or her to buy solar panels for city buildings. The investor agrees. As soon as the solar panels are up, they begin to use the sun to make power. That power is then purchased from the city by PG&E. Pacific Grove takes that money and pays back the investor who bought the panels. In ten to twelve years, the investor is paid off; the panels are up. In the meantime, PG&E is still billing residents as before and using that money to pay back the investor. The investor receives a tremendous tax credit, and PG is generating power from day one. When the debt is finally paid off to the investor, PG owns those panels and becomes its own power company. This would save the city a fortune in power costs, and it's a forced savings account.

I wanted as many people and organizations as possible involved to take advantage of this arrangement. I approached the school superintendent and school board and they were very excited about the project. We created a partnership with the district and discussed how we could buy solar power for his schools and my city buildings, including City Hall, and the police, fire, and public works departments. Through a public/private partnership—schools/city with a private investor—the City could make this happen. They have the design, and the next challenge is to find investors.

Solar power is a resource which I've taken advantage of in my home, and it has reduced my electric bill from $270 a month to $7 a month. Absolutely true.

❐ Saving a Cultural Treasure: Museum of Natural History

As this book goes to print, Pacific Grove, like most cities in the country is having its challenges, one of the most recent being that our treasured Museum of Natural History, established in 1883, was in danger of closing due to lack of funding. However, we actively sought a creative solution to this problem and through a public/private partnership between Pacific Grove and The Museum Foundation, the city council approved a plan that transported the museum from a chrysalis of under-funding and near closure to a revitalized resource with an energetic future. There is hope for all our cities in imaginative, collaborative, and cooperative action.

Community Involvement and Volunteerism

It's important to keep making connections, to keep a flow of communication and action going in all sorts of ways.

For example, I proposed an exhibit for the Pacific Grove Natural History Museum about how the refurbished reservoir would provide water for the golf course and how solar power is used to power buildings. A turnaround isn't just about buildings; it's also about people taking their children to the museum to learn how to keep a city sustainable. We had 570 residents at the museum and taught them how to use green materials and why they shouldn't put certain solvents down their drains. Now, the school wants to adopt the curriculum. The City Council and I worked with the school district on that.

When people are resistant to change or don't think something's possible, you have to show them that it is. I operate my house with solar power; we can operate city buildings the same way. That reservoir worked for years; we can make it work again. You can grow all kinds of food in PG. They used to grow avocados, walnuts, nectarines and lots of fruits here. My wife and I just put a garden in our backyard and we're growing vegetables and blackberries. You can grow your own food too. Modeling the many ways things can change is part of good leadership and good show and tell.

Pacific Grove couldn't run without volunteers. Sometimes they're recruited, or they'll come to the farmer's market or a Sustainable PG meeting, and then they may contact City Hall. An individual might say, "I just moved into town; I'm a filmmaker, and I love historic development." In fact, someone did say that to me. He's thirty-two, a Phi Beta Kappa from Cornell who graduated magna cum laude. He's working on his MBA and a master's degree in Environmental Studies and is fluent in Chinese and Japanese. I appointed him the city planning commissioner. Is he overqualified? Of course, but he loves PG and wants to contribute, and he's great. People come to you.

Summary

You don't become a public servant as an exercise in popularity or because you think people are going to love you or put a statue of you in their storefront. You do it because you love your community. That's your reward. What's important is to leave a place better than you found it.

The renovated old Grove Laundry building, Lighthouse Avenue, provides retail on the first two floors and living quarters for the owners on the top floor. Facing page: Trellis, a garden shop on site, occupies a gazebo made with all recycled materials from the building.

As mayor, I wanted to see people stay in our inns, run in our marathons and visit our butterfly sanctuary. I wanted to maintain our forests and other natural resources and protect the quality of life in the town. My intention was to guide PG to solve its financial problems without capitulating to a Burger King or a similar soulless chain. PG will regain its economic health by, among other things, utilizing its architectural resources more efficiently and thinking more innovatively. That includes creative financing for what we need to build or rebuild and more profit-making ventures for individuals and for the town. I see Pacific Grove becoming a green and self-sustaining community and a revitalized urban village with all the amenities that entails.

Epilogue

"The 20th century was about getting around. The 21st century will be about staying in one place worth staying in."
James Howard Kunstler

The first word of this book is *Imagine*. The first challenge is to see the world, your world, through new eyes. The next is to take action toward transformation within your community.

My hope is that, after having read this book, one person's story—the adventures of a contra-developer—you feel empowered to craft your fortune, your future, your individual vision while becoming a steward of the environment.

I believe the cities of the past hold the keys to the cities of the future as we tackle the challenges of climate change and diminishing resources. They are a last frontier for us—new pioneers—to explore, develop, and re-inhabit. We all must contribute to changes in policy that preserve and utilize our architectural heritage and create new architecture. Fifty percent of our greenhouse gases can be traced to our building practices. Reducing this percentage is one of the most powerful means toward a cleaner, safer environment for ourselves and our children.

I've presented the urban building blocks. Now, I invite you to take your first step—choose a project. Take a walk in your neighborhood, look around, investigate. What could you do here? What do you envision for that empty building? How might the design change? What other transformations might it encourage?

Imagine . . .